Extending offender mobility

Investigating mobile offenders through the case study of 'itinerant crime groups'

Extending offender mobility.

Investigating mobile offenders through the case study of 'itinerant crime groups'

IRCP-series
Volume 43

Stijn Van Daele

Maklu

Antwerpen | Apeldoorn | Portland

An overview of all publications in the IRCP-series is listed at the end of this book.

Stijn Van Daele
Extending offender mobility. Investigating mobile offenders through the case study of 'itinerant crime groups'

Antwerpen | Apeldoorn | Portland
Maklu
2012

155 pag. - 24 x 16 cm
ISBN 978-90-466-0514-1
2012/1997/21
NUR 824

GPRC Guaranteed Peer Reviewed Content www.gprc.be

Maklu-Publishers
Somersstraat 13/15, 2018 Antwerpen, Belgium, info@maklu.be
Koninginnelaan 96, 7315 EB Apeldoorn, The Netherlands, info@maklu.nl
www.maklu.eu

USA & Canada
International Specialized Book Services
920 NE 58th Ave., Suite 300, Portland, OR 97213-3786, orders@isbs.com,
www.isbs.com

Table of contents

Chapter 1. Introduction

1.1 Environmental Criminology, targets and offenders

Crime spans several dimensions. Besides the law, the offender and the target/victim, place can be considered the fourth dimension of crime (Brantingham & Brantingham, 1981a, p. 7). Environmental criminology studies this fourth dimension from several perspectives. Place itself can be considered, for example through the study of criminal hot spots. Other approaches study criminal location choice or the journey-to-crime, emphasising the travelled route and the choices made by offenders. Although objective criteria are important, offender-related elements, such as the anchor point – which refers to the starting point of the crime trip – come into play as well. Further, the interaction between these different criteria is worth of investigation. Thus, environmental criminology is more than just the study of the places and the criminal environment.

One cannot underestimate the importance of place within the study of crime. Sherman (1995) found that the concentration of crime is six times greater among places than it is among persons. As a consequence, he states:

> *"This comparison raises profound questions for both criminological theory and crime control policy. For if future crime is six times more predictable by the address of the occurrence than by the identity of the offender, why aren't we doing more about it? Why aren't we thinking more about wheredunit, rather than just whodunit?"(Sherman, 1995, pp. 36-37)*

Place and movement play an important role in theoretical criminological research. Traditional criminological research has long focused on the individual offender. Already in the nineteenth century scholars studied the role of the city and – more generally – the environment on crime (e.g. Guerry, as referred to in Phillips, 1972, p. 87). Since the 1920s (for example Park, Burgess, McKenzie, & Wirth, 1925) and even more since the 1980s, the study of places has become an important domain of criminological research. For a substantial overview, we refer to Weisburd et al. (2009).

Several theories consider place and its particular characteristics, prominently by looking at routine activities theory. In this theory (Cohen & Felson, 1979;

Felson & Cohen, 1980) it is postulated that crime can only take place when a motivated offender converges in time and space with a suitable target in the absence of a capable guardian. It is the convergence itself that is most important. For example, research of criminal hot spots (see Chainey, 2005; Chainey, Tompson, & Uhlig, 2008; Johnson & Bowers, 2004; Sherman, Gartin, & Buerger, 1989; Weisburd, 2005) studies places where crime often occurs, and in doing so considers the convergence of offenders and targets as well as the role of guardians, thus applying the principles of routine activities theory. Other applications of the principles of routine activity theory deal with police capacity (Groff, 2008, pp. 112-114; Weisburd & Eck, 2004) or situational crime prevention (Mawby, 1977; Newman, 1976; Weisburd, 2004), where guardianship is considered an important element (Reynald, 2009).

Without being too deterministic, the role of place is still underexposed in criminological research (Bottoms & Wiles, 1992, pp. 12-13). People nevertheless consider such elements in their daily routines. A striking example is when people avoid certain places they consider as dangerous or unsafe (Rengert & Pelfrey, 1998). Brantingham and Brantingham (1995, pp. 7-8) divide such crime-prone places into crime generators and crime attractors, providing opportunities for other research on places and their tendencies toward crime. Place clearly has become a worthy domain to study from a criminological perspective. It also does not conflict with more traditional studies on crime, but uses a complementary approach (Eck & Weisburd, 1995, p. 4).

Besides the study of places themselves, one can also consider what makes certain targets more suitable than others. Bernasco and Luykx (2003) identify three elements as highly important in the choice of targets. Targets are likely to be chosen when they are attractive, i.e. the expected profits are high, when the chances of success are high and when the target is easily accessible. These can be studied in an objective sense. Yet, the subjective perception plays a role as well. Referring to opportunity, it is possible that certain houses are intrinsically more interesting to burgle, for example when there is no alarm or visibility from the street is low. Other assessments may compare the target characteristics with features of other potential targets (Bernasco, 2007b, p. 167). The suitability of target X is important as such, but should also be compared with target Y that is located nearby X.

Thus, the features of targets are to be studied within the broader environment in which they are situated. This "broader environment" refers to other potential targets, but can also be influenced by offenders' characteristics. As far as accessibility is concerned, it has been observed that less crime occurs in dead end streets (Beavon, Brantingham, & Brantingham, 1994) – because of the wider accessibility of streets that are not dead ends. Further, not all streets are equally accessible to all offenders. People who, because of their appearance, seem not to belong in a certain neighbourhood, will more likely be regarded as suspicious (Bernasco & Luykx, 2003; Brantingham & Brantingham, 1993b; De Poot, Luykx, Elffers, & Dudink, 2005; Reynald, Averdijk, Elffers, & Bernasco, 2008). Similarly, one may consider a target highly accessible if it is located near one of a city's traffic nodes. Yet, the accessibility for burglar A living nearby may still be different than for burglar B who lives at the other side of town.

This clearly shows that target location choice depends on objective target elements as well as offender characteristics and perception (Bernasco & Nieuwbeerta, 2005, p. 296). Thus, although environmental criminology considers crime within its surroundings, this does not lead to completely disentangling it from the offender.

1.2 Offender mobility

Starting from criminal location choice and considering the relation between targets and offenders, it is only a small step to the next theoretical perspective. According to Cohen and Felson (1979) the convergence of offender and target in time and place is essential for crime to take place. Without convergence, there can be no criminal act. This often requires a certain activity, a distance to be bridged, in other words some mobility.

Strictly speaking, mobility in relation to crime consists of three elements. Criminal mobility can be considered a triangle shaped by: the offender's starting point, the victim's starting point and the crime scene (Groff & McEwen, 2006, pp. 2-3; Rand, 1986; Tita & Griffiths, 2005). These sometimes converge altogether – e.g. in the case of domestic violence – but may also be entirely different – e.g. street robbery.

Movements made by victims have little to do with crime. Although they are necessary for crime to take place, they only consist of trips that are part of daily routines. Hence, criminal mobility is often narrowed down. Instead of the mobility triangle, it looks upon mobility as the movements that are covered by offenders to reach their targets. This interpretation, be it narrow, is also utilised in this work. Thus, criminal mobility refers to an offender's movement to the offence location.

Distance is often a central concept in the study of offender mobility. Yet, other elements come into play as well. Rengert (2004) explicitly mentions the importance not only of distance, but also of the offender's anchor point and the direction of the crime trip. Despite the three-barrelled nature of this concept, distance studies remain predominant in the area of journey-to-crime research.

1.2.1 Basic principles

The basic principle of offender mobility is easy to understand. All other things being equal, offenders are likely to restrict their movements to a minimum. This pattern has already been observed since the first half of the twentieth century. White (1932, p. 507) found offenders in Indianapolis travelled only 2.7 km on average. The same study showed distances travelled to be related to offence type (see also Hesseling, 1992b). Travelled distances for crimes against a person (1.3 km) are shorter than crime trips in the framework of property crime (2.8 km). Several other authors have studied average distances and observed similar numbers and discrepancies. Reppetto (1974) found a mean distance travelled of only 0.8 km for residential burglary. Phillips (1980, p. 175) observed slightly longer trips on average (2.3 km), but also found differences relating to crime type: 1.1 km for assault, 1.7 km for burglary and 4 km for petty larceny. Largely similar were the results of Rhodes and Conly (1981, p. 178), who found averages of 1.8 km for rape, 3.4 km for robbery and 2.6 km for burglaries. In their study on robbery, Capone and Nichols (1975, p. 47) observed crime trips of 5.1 km on average. They concluded that travelled distances are not only influenced by crime type, but also by target type (Capone & Nichols, 1976, p. 209).

One should not only consider offence-related elements – i.e. nature of the offence and target type. Features of the individual offender contribute to offender mobility as well (Bruinsma, 2000, p. 9; 2007, p. 486; Hesseling, 1992a, p. 99). Gabor and Gottheil (1984, pp. 270-271) link three offender characteristics to mobility. They state that young and inexperienced offenders are the least mobile, especially when they belong to a visible minority group (also see Nichols, 1980, pp. 162-163). This group looks particularly suspicious in mainly non-minority neighbourhoods (Bernasco & Block, 2009), hampering them from operating in such neighbourhoods and forcing them to operate near their residence or in other areas where they are not as conspicuous. Young offenders also have few transport options (Reppetto, 1974). If they do not have a driver's licence or a car, they are forced to use other transport methods, making it harder to travel and carry large amounts of loot. Finally, experience is important. During an offender's first five offences the operation area keeps expanding. Afterward they mostly operate within the region they have encountered while travelling for these initial crimes (Barker, 2000). Criminals tend to use efficient movement strategies (see Bernasco, 2007a; Bernasco, 2009; Johnson, Summers, & Pease, 2009). Yet, efficiency is relative to the circumstances each individual offender.

One could argue that these studies are outdated, as mobility in general has seriously extended over the last decades (Bruggeman, 2007, pp. 163-165; Bruinsma, 2000, pp. 3-4; 2004, p. 37; Wiles & Costello, 2000, p. 1). New technologies allow for more, further and quicker movement. Daily examples can be found in the growing cargo trade or the expanding aviation industry. While this applies to mobility in general – for example during work or leisure time – there is little reason to assume that it would be different for crime-related mobility. Nevertheless, the impact is rather modest. Two recent studies on fire setting behaviour found travel distances of 2.1 km (Fritzon, 2001, p. 48) and 6.6 km (Edwards & Grace, 2006, pp. 223-224), respectively, which are in line with the observations of earlier studies. In their Sheffield study on property crime, Wiles and Costello (2000, p. 11) also found rather small crime trips, 3.1 km on average. They even compared the length of crime trips between 1966 and 1995. Although they noticed increased offender mobility, the differences were quite small (Wiles & Costello, 2000, pp. 13, 43). Thus, despite increasing opportunities to travel, many offenders seem to still operate within or in the vicinity of their own neighbourhood.

With the greater part of offences committed near home, other conclusions can be drawn as well. Putting all crimes on a graph results in a rather specific pattern. Most offences are committed near home, followed by a gradual decline in crime rates as distances increase. Due to the nature of this graph, the pattern has been called the distance decay pattern and has been studied by a number of scholars (among others Bernasco, 2006, p. 148; Brantingham & Brantingham, 1981b, p. 33; Canter & Hammond, 2006, p. 97; Canter & Youngs, 2008a, p. 7; Lundrigan & Canter, 2001b, p. 602; Phillips, 1980, pp. 173-174; Rattner & Portnov, 2007, p. 682; Rengert, Piquero, & Jones, 1999, pp. 433-435; Rhodes & Conly, 1981, pp. 178-179; Turner, 1969, p. 13; Van Koppen & Jansen, 1998, p. 231)

The distance decay pattern has also been adopted in police practices. There it serves as one of the keynotes of geographical profiling, where an offender's home area is deduced from the location of his offences (Bernasco, 2004, p. 3; Harries & LeBeau, 2007, pp. 321-322; Rossmo, 1995, 1997; 2000, pp. 188-195). One can then draw a probability model, calculating the chances of an offender living in each area (Rossmo, 2000, p. 207; Van Koppen, Van der Kemp, & De Poot, 2002, p. 247). The applied computer simulations use different mathematical functions to calculate distance decay (Canter & Hammond, 2006, 2007; Kent, Leitner, &

Curtis, 2006). There has been some debate on the accuracy and necessity of such models (Alison, Smith, & Morgan, 2003; Canter, 2005; Paulsen, 2006, 2007; Rossmo, 2005; Snook, Canter, & Bennell, 2002; Snook, Taylor, & Bennell, 2004, 2005), as the complexity of a model does not increase its accuracy (Snook, Zito, Bennell, & Taylor, 2005). One could already achieve some results with just a detailed map and a pair of compasses (Van der Kemp & Van Koppen, 2007; Van Koppen, De Poot, & Van Koppen, 2000; Van Koppen et al., 2002, p. 243). We will not involve ourselves in the discussion about the accuracy of these complex models, but just want to use this example to emphasise that offender mobility is based on a set of relatively simple rules and can be assessed in a straightforward manner.

1.2.2 Differentiations

Although these principles seem very straightforward, they possess a number of differentiations, both technically and regarding content, that complicate them. These complexities cannot always be solved through more sophisticated models. First, several elements transcend the traditional concept of the journey-to-crime. Hence a more accurate interpretation of the information is needed, independent from the technique that has been used. For example one must consider the residence not necessarily as the anchor point. Other aspects are more easily pinpointed through human perception than through computational power. Certain barriers (Brown & Altman, 1981; Elffers, 2004) or facilitating factors – such as traffic nodes (Brantingham & Brantingham, 1984b, p. 357; Fink, 1969; Rossmo, 2000, p. 190) – are easily observed with the naked eye, not needing sophisticated computer models.

1.2.2.1 Distance decay

The distance decay pattern needs differentiation, both regarding its shape and its universal character. In relation to the first aspect, it is said that crime gradually declines with growing distance. However, few or no crimes are committed in the immediate vicinity of an offender's home. There appears a sort of buffer within this area that makes the chance of recognition – or, in other words, the risk –too large to commit crime (Besson, 2004, pp. 193-194; Brantingham & Brantingham, 1981b, p. 32; Rossmo, 1995, pp. 223-224). However, not all authors have observed the existence of such a buffer (Kocsis, Cooksey, Irwin, & Allen,

2002, p. 58). This is probably related to the offence type, as Kocsis et al. (2002) indicate.

A second ongoing debate refers to the applicability of the pattern itself. Van Koppen and De Keijser (1997) designed a model within which the movements of each individual offender show no distance decay, although the aggregated model does. This poses the question of whether distance at the level of individual offenders can be seen as an ecological fallacy. This proposition has been criticised later on by Rengert et al. (1999, pp. 432-433), stating that distance decay has been observed for individual offenders. These findings imply that it is not an ecological fallacy to make statements about this level of analysis, even though throughout the literature conclusions often refer to aggregate data. More recently, this debate has been given new impetus. In a study on burglary, Smith et al. (2009) found a large degree of variation in offender mobility to exist between not as much within individual offenders. Although a general distance decay pattern is observed, this was not demonstrated for individual offenders. Thus, their research confirms the hypothesis that solely representing aggregate data risks losing a rich variation in offender patterns. Investigating these patterns should therefore not involve studying aggregate data alone.

1.2.2.2 The importance of daily routines

Gaining insight into daily routines is crucial for a proper understanding of individual offending patterns. Criminals choose their targets by the information they have acquired over time. They perceive their physical surroundings and, while doing so, create a mental map of the environment (Beauregard, Proulx, & Rossmo, 2005, p. 586; Carter & Hill, 1980; Cromwell, Olson, & Avary, 1991; Kent et al., 2006, p. 197; Nichols, 1980; Rosenbaum & Lavrakas, 1995, p. 10).

The perception of the environment is largely determined by daily behaviour and routines. Brantingham and Brantingham (1981b) call this perception and acquiring of information the awareness space. This space contains all places that are known by an individual (Rengert & Wasilchick, 1985, p. 55) and is developed through both criminal and non-criminal behaviour (Brantingham & Brantingham, 1981b, p. 35; Brantingham & Brantingham, 1984b, pp. 352-355; Brantingham & Brantingham, 1993b; Felson, 2006a, p. 250). These routines not only increase one's knowledge about the places that they have frequented, but also about their surroundings. Likewise, spatial awareness allows offenders to be aware of criminal opportunities (Beavon et al., 1994, p. 117). Experienced offenders in particular have an eye for crime facilitators (Nee & Meenaghan, 2006, p. 937), for example being able to determine whether residents are at home or not (Kleemans, 1996, pp. 53-54).

Not every part of the awareness space contains potential targets. Obviously, there is little value in searching for a suitable target in an area where there no targets exist, or where the risks and profits will always be, respectively, too high and too low. Offenders therefore reduce their search for actual targets to certain areas where suitable targets are encountered (Bernasco & Nieuwbeerta, 2005, p. 297), this narrowed space being called the search space (Rengert & Wasilchick, 1985, p. 55).

A recurrent element that helps to shape the awareness space is residence. Although not always true (Rengert, 2004), the residence is considered the starting point, or the anchor point, of most crime trips. Offenders return to their residences (nearly) every day, thereby systematically constructing knowledge on the immediate neighbourhood. Because this knowledge becomes deep-rooted over time, it even temporarily affects crime patterns after an offender's residence has moved to another area (Bernasco, 2010). Other routines play an important role too: (the road to) work, leisure locations, family and friends' homes. As these movements expand, so does the awareness space, reflecting the link between criminal and non-criminal activities. In both respects, distances travelled are mostly limited (Canter & Youngs, 2008b, pp. 2-3). Moreover, non-criminal behaviour tends to be systematic and situated in large activity nodes like cities. Persons living further away from these areas will likely travel further, both for innocent and criminal purposes. The position with regard to these nodes generates a certain directional bias (Costanzo, Halperin, & Gale, 1986; Rengert & Wasilchick, 1985, p. 69).

1.3 Mobile criminals

Within the criminological literature much is written about confined movement and small distances, which for a long time distracted attention from mobile offenders. In the beginning of the 1980s, McIver frankly stated:

> *"We have, at this time, little empirical basis for specific recommendations to deal with the mobile criminal." (McIver, 1981, p. 44)*

More recently, several authors have mentioned the existence of mobile offenders and expressed a need to investigate them (see Beauregard et al., 2005, p. 591 for an overview). Other authors consider a future general increase in criminal mobility quite conceivable (Bruggeman, 2007).

One should also bear in mind the limited geographic framework considered in most criminological geographical research, often not exceeding the borders of a particular city, for example Philadelphia (Turner, 1969; White, 1932), The Hague (Bernasco, 2006), Perth (Clare, Fernandez, & Morgan, 2009), Norfolk (White, 1999) or Sheffield (Wiles & Costello, 2000). Studies that only consider what happens within one city's boundaries are simply unable to observe larger crime trips. If we assume a city to be circular, then a surface area of 350 km^2 (which is approximately the size of Philadelphia) would not allow us to observe any crime trip longer than 21 km. We do not argue the empirical origin of the distance decay pattern, but this should be no reason to categorically exclude larger distances.

Other scholars do study larger areas and have not excluded crime trips that exceed city borders. Wiles and Costello (2000) compared both approaches. Including the trips of Sheffield offenders that operated outside the city, they found an average of 11 km (Wiles & Costello, 2000, p. 16), while this was only 3.1 km in their intra-city model (Wiles & Costello, 2000, p. 11). Although most offenders operate near their residence, a minority chooses to travel further. Moreover, it is outside the cities in particular that offenders travel further, because there is a different target concentration (Bruggeman, De Ruyver, & Zanders, 1991, p. 64; Clinard, 1944).

Despite a small average, Fritzon (2001, p. 48) observed travel distances of over 100 km in his study on fire setting behaviour. Larger distances have also been found when obtaining drugs (Weir-Smith, 2004, p. 215), and one study on robbery even cited offenders who travelled over 200 km in order to reach their target (1998, p. 231). Examining burglary in the Czech Republic, Polisenska (2008) took things one step further and interviewed offenders who regularly travelled far distances or for whom distance was unimportant. She attributed this to the extensive road network and the Czech habit of frequently travelling to weekend cottages.

The distance decay pattern reveals that most offences are committed near home. Nevertheless, a minority of crimes are committed further away. These crimes too can provide interesting information on the journey-to-crime and offending patterns. According to Rossmo (2000, p. 122), the world is lazy and this includes offenders. Making a rational choice (Cornish & Clarke, 1986b), offenders weigh costs and benefits. The distance decay patterns teach us that this balance will mostly favour short distances. Thus offenders that travel further likely have reasons to do so.

1.3.1 Anchor points

The journey-to-crime is most often calculated by the distance between the offender's residence and the crime scene. One does not even need to know the offender's actual route. Straight-line distances are appropriate in journey-to-crime research and do not require additional functional distance measures for drawing conclusions (Kent et al., 2006).

The impact of the residence is related to the importance of daily routines and central places (Felson, 2006a, pp. 271-272) in criminal behaviour. This approach is mostly suitable for examining offending patterns, however with one major exception. Applying this method to the offender who does not start his crime trip from his residence causes a researcher to incorrectly interpret his mobility. Just like the offence location, the true anchor point should be considered in the analysis of offender mobility (Goodwill & Alison, 2006, p. 408; Rengert, 2004, pp. 169-170; Rossmo, 2000, p. 91). Canter and Larkin (1993) discern two major offending strategies in this respect, giving a central role to circle patterns (Canter & Alison, 2000a; Canter & Gregory, 1994; Canter & Youngs, 2008a, 2008b; Kocsis et al., 2002; Kocsis & Harvey, 1997; Lundrigan & Canter, 2001b; Meaney, 2004; Paulsen, 2007; Sarangi & Youngs, 2006). The first type, called a marauder, departs from home and operates in a circle around his residence. The second type, referred to as a commuter, first moves from his residence to another place, which then functions as the anchor point. While the crimes for the first group are located around the offender's home, the second type possesses another anchor point – often unknown to outsiders – as the centre of the offence locations. The centrality of the residential location (Lundrigan & Canter, 2001a, p. 424) is debatable. The proportion of commuters is also lower for crimes against persons than it is for property crimes, making it more important to study anchor points for this last group (Kocsis & Harvey, 1997, pp. 203-204; Meaney, 2004, pp. 121, 132; Van der Kemp & Van Koppen, 2007, p. 355).

Bearing the awareness space in mind, one may argue that frequently visited places can function as anchor points. It is imperative to not assume the residence is the anchor point from the start. Offenders may well depart from elsewhere, e.g. from work, leisure activities (Brantingham & Brantingham, 1984a), or friends' homes (Wiles & Costello, 2000, p. 40). Even places that play a role in other deviant behavirour, for example locations of drug sales, may function as an anchor point (Rengert, 1992, pp. 111-112). The first offence location of a serial offender is also important, as it constitutes a framework for future crimes (Snook, 2004, p. 54). For co-offenders, it is important to realise that they generally do not commit their crimes in the location of their respective residences, but rather in the surroundings of one of their homes (Bernasco, 2006, p. 147). As a result, the residence is the anchor point for one, but not so for the other(s).

Finally, not all offenders have a fixed residence. Mobile offenders without a stationary home and/or a clear awareness space will follow more complex strategies, making it more difficult to analyse their patterns (Beauregard et al., 2005, p. 591; Bruggeman, 2007, p. 171; Kent et al., 2006, p. 187; Rossmo, 1995; 2000, p. 223; Tittle & Paternoster, 1988).

1.3.2 True mobility

Incorrect interpretation of the anchor point constitutes a first possible explanation of – seemingly – high mobility. Although travelling to a crime takes time, effort and money (Pettiway, 1982, p. 257) it is sometimes worthwhile, even if there is no additional anchor point to keep down costs. This could be the result of extensive planning in order to reduce the risk (Capone & Nichols, 1975, p. 48; 1976, p. 203; Mawby, 2001, p. 72). Criminals who thoroughly plan their crimes, are less confined to their awareness space and daily routines (Rhodes & Conly, 1981, p. 178). Planning therefore results in longer crime trips (Laukkanen & Santtila, 2006, p. 71; Laukkanen, Santtila, Jern, & Sandnabba, 2008, p. 226), although it alone is not a sufficient explanation. After all, planning itself is an extra effort. The relationship between criminal planning and the length of the crime trip should be considered in the light of risks and profits. On the one hand offences that are planned in detail often require this preparation in order to have any chance of success, for example robberies and kidnappings. Not all potential targets lend themselves to these types crimes. Offenders often have to travel further to find a suitable target at all (Van Koppen & Jansen, 1998, pp. 232-233)

On the other hand these crimes generate more profits if they are successful. Higher earnings make up a key issue in the relation between planning and mobility. Offenders are likely to travel further when the expected profits are higher (Buettner & Spengler, 2001, p. 18; Snook, 2004, p. 62). As already mentioned, these higher profits can be the result of the offence type, but even for other crimes – including those that do not require extensive planning by nature – is mobility related to more earnings (Morselli & Royer, 2008, p. 12).

One should also take into account the nature of much of the data on offender mobility. Most studies on movement of offenders use either police data or interviews with convicted offenders. These data only refer to solved crimes and have thus already passed a first filter. One hypothesis is that mobile offenders are less likely to be arrested. Their mobility makes it easier for them to stay out of sight of the authorities, therefore they are less often recorded in crime statistics (Eck & Weisburd, 1995; McIver, 1981, p. 43). This methodological shortcoming of most existing research would then fortify the distance decay patterns. This advantage of higher mobility transcends the traditional methods of measuring mobility. Whereas a wrong interpretation of the anchor point causes an overestimation of mobility, the reverse is true here, methodological shortcomings underestimating travelled distances.

1.3.3 Examples of mobile offenders

Most criminological research focuses on local offending patterns. In the previous section we have already mentioned that this is not a universal pattern. A number of variations to this basic principle were brought up. The following section discusses some more precise examples mobile offenders.

1.3.3.1 Dacoities

A first example of mobile offenders is found India, and began 2500 years ago. Rossmo (1995, pp. 220-221; 2000, pp. 188-189) describes dacoities as gangs of mobile robbers within India's caste system. They operated in groups of five or more persons. Due to the lack of anonymity in the rural areas where they stayed (see also Clinard, 1944), they decided to travel to other villages to commit crimes. They mainly operated when there was little moonlight. Moreover, they had to return home by the time the early farmers started working in their fields. Although they had few opportunities – they rarely had any transport at their disposal and could only operate in a short time span – they managed to travel quite large distances, making it more difficult to trace them.

1.3.3.2 *Goat riders*

A second group of mobile offenders is found in Western Europe. During the eighteenth century, the so-called Goat riders, or "bokkenrijders", plagued what are now northeast Belgium and the southeast part the Netherlands (Limburg). These offenders operated in groups and were responsible for a number of bare-faced robberies, targeting large farms and presbyteries (Blok, 1992). Because of the use of excessive violence, their crimes left seriously wounded and murdered victims. The reaction of the judicial authorities was correspondingly severe (De Ruyver, 2001). The groups committed crimes in large areas, provoking the imagined belief that they would travel by goats through the air at night (Naus, 2008), hence their name. Most of the Goat riders belonged to families of skinners (Blok, 1992; Crott, 1990). This profession enjoyed little prestige, positioning these people on the fringes of society. Moreover, they were unable to find steady jobs, forcing them to move from one region to the other. This created even more difficulties in fitting in with the local population. This helps to understand their similarly large mobility during their offences.

These groups were punished severely both for the violence they used and partly due to their social status. Under torture, offenders gave away more names of other offenders than actually existed. They also confessed to more crimes than they actually committed. In this way, the perception of this crime phenomenon transcended its true proportions (Augustus, 2000). These offenders' mobility can be attributed to their temporary anchor points. This was enhanced as their social status and isolation led to little social control from other groups (Van de Bunt & Kleemans, 2007, pp. 79-80).

1.3.3.3 *Kappa gangs*

Also in Western Europe, a new type of mobile offender groups appeared at the end of the 1980s and the beginning of the 1990s. They were called Kappa gangs. These offenders committed property crimes in a violent, nearly military style (Vermeulen, De Busser, & Cruysberghs, 2003, p. 221). They particularly targeted shops and used fast cars and motorways and major highways to move between Belgium and France (Bruggeman et al., 1991, p. 37). This made it possible to be at the crime site for a very short period. Other researchers have already pointed at the importance of these roads in assessing the patterns of mobile offenders (see Brantingham & Brantingham, 1984b, p. 357; Fink, 1969; Rossmo,

2000, p. 190). Because of their swiftness, they were rarely deterred by witnesses or alarms (Bruggeman et al., 1991, p. 133). Additionally, their large operation area hampered linking particular crimes to certain gangs (Bruggeman et al., 1991, p. 142).

1.3.3.4 Rich pickings

Another sample of mobile offenders is found in what Mawby (2001, pp. 71-72) calls rich pickings. In contrast to the three previously discussed phenomena, the specific character of these offenders is less marked. The difference lies more in the target choice. These offenders aim at maximising risk, whereas other offenders are more likely to limit risk (Felson, 2002, p. 39).

Generally speaking, most burglaries are committed in less affluent areas (Johnson & Bowers, 2004, p. 238; Malczewski & Poetz, 2005, p. 523; Rengert & Wasilchick, 1985, p. 60). Ethnographic research in the beginning of the 1980s also reveals another typology of offenders. Maguire (1982) investigates certain burglars operating in Gerrards Cross, a residential place situated in London's green belt that can be reached easily over a number of arterial roads. Burglars operating here are mostly highly experienced and use accomplices for the job. They obtain high earnings through their crimes and have often already been convicted in several districts. Unlike offenders who commit crimes in their daily routines, these rich pickers deliberately choose to head for potential targets mainly situated in rural areas. They tend to be more interested in potential gains than in the proximity of the target (Cohen & Cantor, 1981, pp. 123-124). They generate their own criminal opportunities, so to speak, by actively seeking potential targets. Hence, this typology is also called *the search* (Bennett & Wright, 1984, p. 45) and, as these offenders often travel far, even the expression *journeymen* (Cromwell et al., 1991, p. 50) has been used.

1.3.3.5 Itinerant criminals

Since the second half of the 1990s, a new typology of mobile offenders have appeared in Western Europe: groups of criminals coming over from Eastern Europe who systematically – and often in sprees – commit property crimes and are highly mobile in their operations. In Belgium they are called itinerant crime groups (De Ruyver, 2006b; Ponsaers, 2004), in the Netherlands mobile bandits

(Van der Laan & Weenink, 2005). Recently, awareness of these offender groups is expanding across many countries in the European Union (Van Geffen, 2009).

Until now, most attention to this group has come from law enforcement agencies. Academic research focusing on these groups is limited, but certain scholars have discussed similar offenders (see Bovenkerk, 2001; Spapens & Fijnaut, 2005; Van San, Snel, & Boers, 2002).

The mobility of these offenders can be considered in two ways. First, they travel from Eastern to Western Europe and many exclusively use temporary residences. They can be considered itinerant because of this mobile lifestyle (see Macdonald, 1993). Second, research by police authorities (De Cock, 2006b, p. 22).has found that these offenders have a large operation area as well, travelling 35 km on average with peaks of over 150 km and operating on both sides of national borders (Spapens & Fijnaut, 2005, pp. 83-84). Similar to other mobile offenders, they often use major highways to travel during their crimes (De Raedt, 2005, p. 21; De Raedt, Henin, Wick, Libois, & Rokegem, 2007, p. 13; Vervaet & Willems, 2006, p. 12).

1.4 Structure of the book

Limited offender mobility is considered the rule in most criminological research. Mobile offenders follow a deviating pattern and can be studied as an atypical case study (Denscombe, 1998, p. 33; Gerring, 2007, pp. 105-108). When the aim is to study the most often occurring patterns, it can be problematic to examine extreme cases (McKeown, 2004, p. 147). Further, the study of offender mobility is often restricted to local offenders and, by studying only crime trips that start and end within a certain area, excludes mobile criminals (see Wiles & Costello, 2000 for the consequence of this method). The concepts that have been developed concerning offender mobility are therefore only applied to local criminals.

Although we do not question the existence of this pattern of distance decay, there are reasons to study mobile offenders as well. One can only be sure that the developed concepts and principles do sufficiently fit in with the study of criminals and their movements if mobile offenders are included in the analysis. In this introductory chapter, we have discussed some exceptions that refine the general perception of local offending. All other things being equal, offenders choose nearby targets. Yet, "all other things" are often not equal, creating incentives for offenders to travel. Both methodological misconceptions and true reasons for travelling have also been addressed.

Unlike McIver (1981, p. 44) and despite the methodological difficulties (Brantingham & Brantingham, 1984b; Rossmo, 2000) this embodies, we believe there are reasons to study mobile criminals, which we discuss in the following chapters. First, there is mobility itself. How mobile are these "mobile" offenders and is this large mobility reflected in the distance decay pattern as well? In other words, do mobile offenders show different, if any at all, distance decay than local offenders do? Second, attention needs be given to the mechanisms that make offenders travel. One of the obvious and tangible examples is the shift in profits, whether it is because of the crime type itself or not. Other features may relate to the target (area) too. How do the risks shift between nearby and far targets, and do any other methods enhance mobile offending? Yet, one should also look beyond the crime itself. Therefore, the anchor point should be assessed in order to find out whether these offenders use nearby alternative starting points that make us overestimate their crime trip. Finally, we also consider the awareness space and how this relates to mobile offending.

Particularly focusing on itinerant criminals as a case study of mobile offenders, the aim of this book is not to calculate certain effects, but to reveal and understand the mechanisms that do account for large criminal mobility (Gerring, 2007, pp. 43-48). This does not falsify the reigning understanding of the principles applicable to local offenders. However, it may refine the application of some of these principles to offender mobility in general. Mobile offenders are not new. During history, several typologies of mobile offenders have been observed, itinerant crime groups being just one of them.

In chapter 2, the concept of itinerant crime groups and the various ways of data sampling are explained. The study made use of police statistics, case files and offender interviews. Each one of them is described and the choices are explained. As most chapters are based on papers that have already been published elsewhere, the occurrence of some repetition of information is inevitable. The main recurring issue in these papers was the conceptualisation of 'itinerant crime groups' and the methodology. To largely reduce repetition, these aspect are covered once.

The following chapters describe our own empirical findings about these groups and their mobility, both in a quantitative and in a qualitative. The phenomenon of offender mobility and the characteristics ascribed to it in Belgium are empirically tested. In chapter 3, we find that the features of mobility and nationality emerge as useful characteristics by which to study these crime groups. There are no indications that the special character of these groups is the consequence of policy-related attention, but rather it functions as a catalyst for interest.

Chapter 4 expands mobility beyond average distances travelled and considers these offenders' distance decay functions. It finds that Eastern European multiple offending groups tend to commit their crimes in rural areas. Although they start their journey in regions considered "crime importing", they carry out their crimes in "crime exporting" areas. As such, they are atypical, challenging traditional theories on journey-to-crime, being into question the way in which police forces are organised.

In chapter 5, we empirically investigate 'itinerant crime groups' and the key issues that make them special. By analysing 27 case files, a large degree of variation is revealed. Groups differ in size, organisational structure, offender characteristics, the crimes in which they are involved and the methods they use. According to these features, two main types of itinerant crime groups can be distinguished, each with their own diversity. As a result, the observed heterogeneity is larger than we might suspect by looking at the policy definition of the phenomenon.

After these descriptive chapters, a more explanatory approach is taken. Explanations for mobility can be both methodological and empirical. Chapter 6 again takes a quantitative approach as it contributes to the discussion on the individual application of distance decay. Although near-home offending has also been observed at the individual offender level, it has been debated whether distance decay actually exists at this level as well. We therefore believe it is important to distinguish near-home offending from decay, i.e. the gradual decline in offences as distances increase. This chapter studies mobility patterns and decay curves in serious property crimes in Belgium. First, aggregated patterns are discussed and categorised. Second, individual offenders are analysed. It becomes clear through studying offender patterns that offender mobility and decay are not intertwined at the individual level to the same extent as they are at the aggregate level. This suggests that it is important, particularly when studying individual offenders, to clarify whether (average) distances or decay are being considered.

Chapter 7 also considers mobility patterns from a methodological point of view, but now a qualitative one. One hypothesis concerning the crime travelling behaviour of itinerant crime groups is that they do not have fixed residences, hence creating the – incorrect – image of them travelling larger distances. The central question of this chapter is therefore whether high offender mobility is a result of anchor point flexibility. While home is often considered the logical anchor point of crime travelling behaviour, this could eventually be proven incorrect. Looking at a number of case files, an initial glance is taken at the interpretation of the anchor point for these groups:the question arising here is whether a case-to-case interpretation of these anchor points offers an explanation for the distances travelled. Although residences of itinerant crime groups are not always easy to determine, the results indicate that these groups do indeed travel large distances. This is still the case when the anchor points of these groups are studied more thoroughly.

In chapter 8, we cross the bridge of possible methodological shortcomings of mobility measures towards the rationale for criminal mobility. This section goes beyond city boundaries and discusses 'outbound offenders', whose crime trips start in a city, but end outside. It is argued that a substantial proportion of crime trips follow this pattern, indicating that areas other than cities also provide interesting opportunities for property crime. We find that outbound offending mostly occurs towards affluent target regions and near motorways, which confirms findings from previous research. We also find crime sprees to be indicative for mobile offending. Thus, mobile property offenders tend to compensate for travelled distances, not only by targeting affluent areas and using fast transportation means, but also by committing several successive offences, hereby reducing their relative transportation cost for each offence. Although this chapter does not refer to methodological shortcomings in assessing offender mobility, it is of methodological relevance, in particular with respect to offender mobility studies in general. This chapter shows that, while much attention is paid to offending and offender mobility within cities, it is worthwhile to consider other patterns too.

In Chapter 9, we apply several explanations of offender mobility to itinerant crime groups. Using crime statistics, case file analysis and offender interviews we find mobility is compensated for in various ways. We first looked into some possible target-oriented explanations, which, although they did reveal useful information, was not sufficient to explain the differences between itinerant crime groups and other property offenders. Offender related explanations provide an additional explanatory value, but not exclusively. Awareness space is also considered. Reconnaissance activities, repeat victimisation, target type familiarity and even the use of maps help to develop their geographical knowledge. Some information could not be exclusively attributed to either target or offender related issues. Furthermore, the offender's awareness space plays a crucial role in offending patterns. This refers to all spaces of which an offender has knowledge developed through daily routines. Our findings suggest that the understanding of the role of awareness space should be differentiated from its traditional understanding. Spatial awareness does not only provide opportunities for crime, but can actually limit it at times.

This book may be of interest for different kinds of readers. Taking into account each one's background and, different chapters may be of particular interest. All readers may want to read or at least skim chapter 2, as it sets out the basic notions for the rest of the book, both concerning methodology and the concept of 'itinerant crime groups'. Police practitioners interested in the phenomenon of itinerant crime groups may afterwards prefer to read chapters 3, 4, 5 and 9 while criminologists with an interest in offender mobility may find more pleasure in going through chapter 4, followed by a reading of the last four chapters (6 to 9). Within these groups, some may feel more acquainted with quantitative methods, while others prefer a qualitative assessment of the problem. The first group will probably find chapters 6 and 8 most appealing, while the latter group may prefer to read chapters 5, 7 and 9. Chapters 3 and 4 contain some quantitative analysis although readers with a quantitative background may find it rather unchallenging and also people with a more qualitative background will be able to understand most that has been described. Thus, depending on their time available, readers may prefer to either skip, skim or completely read those chapters.

This book is inspired by contributions which have appeared in a number of scientific journals. The added value of the book lies in a number of factors. First, the papers have been revised for the purpose of this book, some analyses have been added, extended or left out for a larger consistency throughout the book. Second, it puts together various findings and involves a heterogeneous overview of criminological studies that extend the traditional perception of offender mobility.

Chapter 2. Concepts and methods

2.1 Itinerant crime groups

Since the late 1990s, Belgian law enforcement agencies have noticed an increasing number of offenders (Dupuis, 2004) who are engaging in "regular" property crimes, but with higher levels of mobility. Instead of staying around their residence, these groups choose to travel further during their criminal operations. Because of the mobility of these offenders, they have been called "itinerant crime groups" (De Ruyver, 2006a). After half a decade of fine-tuning, the phenomenon was defined and recorded in Belgian criminal policy, in the so-called *Kadernota Integrale Veiligheid (2004)*. The key features of systematic offending, group offending, Eastern European origin and operation from the main Belgian cities or abroad, were assigned to these groups. Another key feature is their high level of mobility. Due to their levels of mobility, the activities of these groups seem to conflict with general observations concerning limited offender mobility. Furthermore, they challenge some common principles of police management and organization. Mobile criminals create a need for police forces to cooperate, share their knowledge and conduct joint investigations. The fact that this now occurs for rather "ordinary" property crimes may cause a shift in the organization of police activities.

Media coverage indicates that these offenders have a large impact on the Belgian criminal landscape. Between 60 and 80 such groups have been identified each year in Belgium since 2004 (De Raedt, 2006b). The size of these groups changes, indicating that their structure is flexible, and the organisations have become smaller (De Raedt, 2006b, p. 41). An overview of the case files reveals a large variety of groups. Some only comprise around five offenders, while others have more than 70 members. The number of offences committed range from a couple of dozens to, exceptionally, more than 1,000 crimes. More recently, the number of groups that are registered annually has been increasing. Although this may have something to do with growing police attention as well, the international picture indicates the problem is certainly not diminishing.

Policies concerning these crime groups, and how to define their members, were updated by the government in two revised action plans (2007; 2010). The latter has been translated in English and was released shortly before the Belgian presidency of the European Union. As such, it contributed to a large extent in

Belgians efforts to put this criminal phenomenon on the political agenda. According to this action plan, an itinerant criminal group is an association of offenders:

- which systematically commits burglaries in houses, in companies or shops, including ram-raids, cargo thefts, metal thefts and thefts of heavy equipment (on construction sites);
- whose members mainly originate from the former Eastern bloc countries or form a sedentary group of offenders in Belgium;
- which operates or is directed from abroad or from the big urban areas in Belgium;
- which commits a considerable number of offences in a large part of the territory and;
- sometimes exploits minors for committing thefts.

However, this definition does not exclude that an itinerant criminal group can also be involved in other offences, such as armed robbery, car- and home-jacking, theft of valuable documents, trafficking in vehicles, theft with ruse, organised pick-pocketing, organised shoplifting and skimming.

Compared with the initial definition in 2004, increasing attention has been paid to so-called "sedentary" groups: offenders that belong to communities with a long history of a travelling lifestyle, but who have more recently settled in vulnerable communities in Western European cities. From there and using the high levels of anonymity in these neighbourhoods, they engage in criminal activities. Typical for these offenders is the use of minors in criminal activities. Children are sent out for a variety of crimes including begging, pickpocketing, shoulder surfing at ATM machines, theft with ruse, shoplifting, burglaries,...

Organised property crime by these groups is raising concerns not only in Belgium, but also in some of its neighbouring countries, under a variety of names. Already in the beginning of the 21st century, the Netherlands, France and Germany focused on these groups, which were labelled, respectively, 'mobile banditism' (Huisman & Van der Laan, 2005; Van der Laan & Weenink, 2005) 'itinerant crime' (Marro, 2002) and 'Eastern European criminal groups' (Dortans, 2007).

More recently, many other countries have become aware of this criminal phenomenon, such as the United Kingdom, Spain, Italy, Austria and Switzerland, the Scandinavian countries, and Czech Republic (Van Geffen, 2009, pp. 19-23).

In many of these countries a defining element of these groups is that they systematically commit property offences. By committing property crime, these groups connect organised crime – or, at least, group offending – with crimes that may have a large impact on the daily lives of regular citizens. Contrary to more traditional types of 'organised crime' – drug trafficking, trafficking in human beings,... – these criminals target the belongings of citizens, companies and vulnerable groups. Estimates indicate the loss suffered by the European retail sector due to these groups would amount to EUR7.6billion annually (Van Geffen, 2009).

Engagement in property crimes, however, does not make them completely different from other criminal gangs or organisations. Spapens and Fijnaut (2005, p. 82) distinguish four offender types in their study on organised burglary. Next to itinerant crime groups –or mobile gangs– as they call them, 'professional thieves' may also operate in groups and/or work in organised structures. The same concerns car theft and smuggling of stolen vehicles, another example of property crimes executed by criminal groups (Bruinsma & Bernasco, 2004, p. 86; Spapens & Fijnaut, 2005, p. 98). Then what is it that makes these so-called 'itinerant crime groups' this special? Although the choice of words varies to describe these groups, mobility is a recurrent issue. As described in the introduction, criminological research has found that most offences are committed in the vicinity of the offender's home. For itinerant crime groups, however, this is not the case. These offenders travel further than other offenders, not only by travelling throughout Europe, but also during their criminal offences.

Scientific publications on these groups have been rather limited and, until the development of the present study, even exceptional (e.g. Ponsaers, 2004 for one example). Yet, some publications assess the phenomenon from a different perspective – or at least without using the term 'itinerant crime groups'. They focus on burglary by Yugoslavian gangs (e.g. Bovenkerk, 2001; Van San et al., 2002) or crime by travelling communities (Macdonald, 1993). Although the European context creates a large focus on Eastern European offenders from this perspective, a similar phenomenon has been studied in the United States, where the focus lies on 'South American theft groups'. Mentioned countries of origin are Colombia, Chile, Peru, Ecuador, Venezuela and Mexico (Caputo, 2008).

Next to the theoretical implications this involves, they also challenge some common principles of police management and organization. Mobile criminals create a need for police forces to cooperate, share their knowledge and conduct joint investigations. The fact that this now occurs for rather "ordinary" property crimes may cause a shift in the organization of police activities. As a result of this mobility and given the implications for police operations, the Dutch police has particularly started to focus on all criminal networks that operate not on a local, but on a regional, national or even international level (Korps Landelijke Politiediensten, 2008, p. 146). Yet, such operations on group level does not exclude the involvement of local offenders. As Fijnaut (1998) has described, there is a difference between the transnational nature of crime and the transnational character of criminals committing these crimes. Transnational criminal activities may largely involve locally oriented offenders with only one or two transnationally oriented perpetrators (Bruinsma & Bernasco, 2004) or vice versa. For these groups, it appears the activities are largely not international – property crimes generally require no border-crossing – but the offenders are.

Estimating the number of crimes committed by these groups is almost impossible. Mobility in itself is not a crime. The crimes that are committed are crimes – property crimes such as residential burglaries, metal thefts, commercial burglaries – that are not the exclusive domain of these groups. Hence, one can only be sure that crimes have been committed by mobile offenders if they are caught. For other crimes, one can only judge the probability by method of operation, target choice or other elements, but there is no certainty at all.

The reader will by now have noticed that the definition of the phenomenon and the identification of its size can be interpreted in several ways. The criminal phenomenon we are dealing with is not straightforward to study. Still, the mobility patterns that are ascribed to it appear too special to leave it aside. To study the phenomenon in its heterogeneity, several methods, each with their own focus, have been incorporated. Furthermore, such an approach allows to combine several approaches: quantitative and qualitative, target-oriented and offender-oriented, descriptive and explanatory.

2.2 Methodology

In the framework of this study, three main methods have been used. Police statistics are used for exploring the extent of this phenomenon, quantitative analysis and for achieving an overall image of offender mobility and crime involvement. Furthermore, this method allows for a comparison with other offenders involved in property crime. Case file analysis has further helped to get more insight in the structures of these groups and obtain information that is not incorporated in the police statistics. Finally, offender interviews are added to understand the offenders' general background and motivations behind certain offending patterns, in this way transcending pure crime data. As such, the three methods complement each other. Quantitative and general findings (police statistics) are supplemented with more in-depth information, more precise patterns with respect to criminal activities (case file analysis and interviews) and even general background information (interviews).

2.2.1 Police statistics

A first major source consists of police statistics of serious property crimes – i.e. all property crimes with aggravating circumstances such as breaking and entering or the use of violence. We chose not to focus on one crime type in particular as offenders are relative generalists who do not solely engage in one type of crime (Felson, 2006a, p. 235). The confinement to serious property crimes was prompted by the fact that these are the crimes in which itinerant crime groups are active, according to the definition

After requiring the necessary permissions, these data were extracted from the ANG, which is the Dutch abbreviation for 'General national database'. ANG forms the most important and uniform database for nationwide police statistics in Belgium. Because the project started in 2007, we obtained data from the years 2002 to 2006. Information on offender mobility can only be obtained if the offender of a certain crime is known. This formed another restriction of our data. Given the nationwide scope of the data and focus on all serious property crimes, a large dataset has been generated, including 87,383 crimes and 64,409 offenders. Offenders may commit several crimes and crimes may be committed by several offenders. We therefore used offender-offence combinations as the unit of analysis (e.g. Hodgson & Costello, 2006; Kleemans, 1996), giving us over 140,000 units to analyse.

Throughout the book, mobility has mostly been measured by calculating the distances between offence site and the offender's residence. Hence, only those offenders were considered who had a residence registered in the database. This operation reduced the dataset to about half its size. Furthermore, foreign residences caused additional problems and suffered from two major flaws in particular. First, no detailed information other than the country was provided. The margin of error this generates is quite large for our neighbouring countries. It is impossible to determine whether an offender living in France started in Paris or very close to the Belgian border. While his mobility in the last case could be quite limited – when he operates in the border region – this is not the case when he started in Paris or even further down south. For offenders living in other countries, this is less problematic. For an offender living in Lithuania, it does not really matter where exactly in Lithuania he started: his mobility is still over 1,500km, even when he started close to the border with Poland. Yet, for such offenders another problem arises. Even if they have their residence in their country of origin, it is highly unlikely they have actually started their crime trip over there. They will probably have a secondary anchor point in Belgium, which in that case is not registered in the database.

For these reasons, the traditional calculation of crime trips does not consider residences abroad (as was the case for about 7% of the sample). Together with the exclusion of the offenders for whom no residence was known, the final sample contains just above 68000 offender-offence combinations. For one analysis, offender mobility is measured through criminal range. In that case it is not necessary to eliminate certain offenders and even offenders whose residence is unknown are included in the analysis.

Subsequently, the locations were geocoded using the Lambert 1972 projection, which is quite common in Belgium. Due to the sample size, it was beyond the project's financial resources to have all individual addresses geocoded. Alternatively, the geographic centre of each of Belgium's 589 municipalities is used. Because of this size, such a method ignores the existing tendency to work on an ever more detailed level of analysis. This tendency has been facilitated by recent technological evolutions. Furthermore, focusing on smaller units of analysis better explains people's individual choices (Oberwittler & Wikström, 2009).

The approach used here uses 589 geographic units. In their plea for using smaller geographic units, Oberwittler and Wikström (2009, p. 35) use 550 geographic areas. Thus, the number of units as such is not problematic in the present study. Yet, it does use another scale – nationwide data instead of the much more accepted citywide patterns. As we focus on mobile offenders, this is an acceptable choice. Still, it hampers comparisons with other, more traditional studies of citywide offending patterns

Using the municipalities' centres has another advantage. Particularly regarding rural areas, the geographic midpoint of an area largely corresponds with the larger concentration of targets in the administrative centre of these regions. Finally, one may argue that the study of municipalities adds further knowledge to the findings that originate from studies focusing on neighbourhood level analysis in understanding geographic crime patterns (Hardyns & Pauwels, 2009; Pauwels, 2002; Van de Velde, Pauwels, & Hardyns, 2009).

To calculate crime trips, the Euclidian distances between the centres are used. Euclidian distances actually underestimate the real travel path or travel time

(Gabor & Gottheil, 1984, p. 273). Yet, it is mostly the most accurate measurement (Kent et al., 2006, p. 194).

In case the residence and offence location are situated in the same area – something that occurs regularly (see also Brantingham & Brantingham, 1993b, p. 20), distances are estimated using a formula that is also used by Bernasco (2006, p. 147):

$$\frac{\sqrt{Surface\ area}}{2}$$

Consequently, target variables used in this analysis refer to the values – affluence, population density, ... – that correspond with the respective area.

Briefly spoken, the used method largely corresponds with those used in similar publications. Yet, the present study increases the scale of the study: neighbourhood characteristics become municipality characteristics in the present study, neighbourhood centres become municipality centres and the study's total scope is not one city but a whole nation.

The broad interpretation of 'itinerant crime groups' in policy documents makes it rather difficult to put the definition into operation for empirical research. After all, 'itinerant crime groups' have increasingly become a catch-all term for organised property crimes. Yet, the extent of 'organisation' is not clearly defined either. In this book, an offender-oriented approach has mainly been used, although only criminals committing property crimes are considered. Offender-oriented approaches have evolved over the last decades. Whereas research into criminal organisations has a tradition of focusing on well-structured groups, more criminologists have started to study offenders as members of flexible social networks with an organic way of cooperation (Black, Vander Beken, Frans, & Paternotte, 2001; Bruinsma & Bernasco, 2004; Easton & Karaivanov, 2009; McIllwain, 1999; Morselli & Tremblay, 2004; Ruggiero, 1996, pp. 5-6; Shelley, 1999; Van Calster, 2002; Von Lampe, 2001, 2004). The image of the vertically organised criminal organisation has been superseded and some criminologists argue there is little to no added value in using large groups for most criminal operations at all (Felson, 2002, p. 10; 2006b, p. 16). Hence, paying only attention to groups with a rather fixed structure and division of tasks would be too narrow.

'Itinerant crime groups' are defined as having the following five key features: they commit property crime, offences are committed systematically, the criminals act as a group or 'association', they come from Eastern European countries and they are more mobile than other offenders. These four features are adopted from the definition. The first condition, property crimes, is met by the nature of our data.

The second, systematic commitment of offences, was put into operation by using multiple offending. The conditions for 'multiple offences' are either a limited number of offences for which the criminal was convicted, or a more substantial number of registered contacts with the police authorities, without the requirement of conviction. Wartna and Tollenaar (2004, p. 34) refer to criminals as 'multiple offenders' in case of at least three criminal trials during a 5-year time span. A similar approach is found with Lovegrove (2000, p. 454), who defines multiple offenders as criminals who have been convicted at least two times for crimes that are not linked to one another. Furthermore, a certain threshold of seriousness is set. Such an approach cannot be used in the present study as we are dealing with police data. Hence, no information is given on the eventual outcome of the investigations in court.

Elffers (2003) uses a slightly different understanding of multiple offending. He abandons the need for a conviction and focuses on precedents in police data. These contain every criminal report against a suspect of one or several crimes. This broadens the chances of offenders being included, as such a report can be filed, even if the suspect turns out innocent afterwards. To compensate for the larger number of false positives, he levels the minimum threshold from two or five to ten precedents.

Other authors use this approach as well (Ferwerda, Versteegh, & Beke, 1995). Initially, this approach was used for categorising juvenile offenders. Those who were suspected of committing more than ten crimes were distinguished from those who had between three and ten precedents and those who had less (Versteegh, Janssen, & Bernasco, 2003). Yet, over time this approach has been increasingly cut loose from juvenile delinquency and used for other offenders as well (Ferwerda, Kleemans, Korf, & Van der Laan, 2003, p. 112). In the case of offences that do not result in conviction, ten registered contacts is a recurrent condition. Given the nature of our data, the second approach fits best.

In relation to the third factor, that of criminals acting as a group, co-offending (Weerman, 2001, 2003) was considered for two reasons. First, the data allowed no interpretation of group structure. Thus, no information on size and organisations could be linked to the data. Furthermore, no precise definition of 'association' has been used. Doing so in this study would squeeze us right in between the various approach advocating group (vertical vs horizontal orientation) structures or criminal networks (Canter & Alison, 2000b; Easton & Karaivanov, 2009) which may also vary over time and in relation to crime types (Bruinsma & Bernasco, 2004). Furthermore, co-offending itself may as well influence criminal patterns to an extent that is largely underestimated (Andresen & Felson, 2010; Felson, 2003), for example concerning criminal earnings (Morselli, Tremblay, & McCarthy, 2006) and mobility (Bernasco, 2006).

Fourth, special attention was paid to Eastern European offenders. The police data do not contain any information on origin, but only nationality. As Eastern European, those offenders were considered who had a nationality of one of the former Soviet states, the Soviet satellite states (the so-called Eastern Bloc) or the Balkan region. We are aware that the relationship between nationality and crime is a complex one and should not lead to criminal branding of certain communities (Garland & Chakraborti, 2007; James, 2007; Piquero & Brame, 2008). Hence it is important to realised that this study does not make any statements on the relationship between certain nationalities and crime as such. What it does handle is the relationship between nationality and mobility patterns. Furthermore, as we will observe later on, even this relationship is not taken for granted without empirical analysis.

The fifth and final element – mobility – was not assumed as necessary condition. Despite the seeming contradiction this embodies, this is done in order to avoid tautology. After all, the first part of the book aims at finding out whether these groups are indeed more mobile than other criminals. If we would only include mobile offenders in our analysis, we would obviously find them to be more mobile than others. Moreover, mobility can vary for individual offenders: an offender may commit most of his crimes near home, but this does not mean he may also commit offences far away or the other way around. Although one can of course calculate mean travelled distances for each offender, mobility is related to each individual offence. It is neither related to offenders themselves nor to fixed patterns, unlike other features as Eastern European origin, multiple offending and group operations.

Thus, in the police data, itinerant crime groups were put into operation as follows:

- Property offenders
- Co-offenders
- Having committed ten or more crimes
- Being citizens of an Eastern European country

2.2.2 Case file analysis

A second additional data source consists of 27 criminal case files of so-called itinerant crime groups. This method allows to further deepen the knowledge of structures and mobility patterns of these groups. Particular attention is herewith paid to the groups' anchor points. Furthermore, relevant case file information is used understand and triangulate some mechanisms that are already partly discovered through the analysis of police data. Contacts were made with judicial police forces in five districts with various features: geographic location, size, degrees of urbanisation and whether the district mainly functions as target area or more as a starting point. As such, a maximum degree of diversity is being aimed for, in order to grasp the heterogeneity of itinerant crime groups. In this method, we could dig deeper than just nationality concerning the origin of these groups, giving us the opportunity to incorporate the sedentary groups from the definition too.

The first district is located at the Belgian coastline near the French border. In this district, a number of groups have been active, both Eastern European and French sedentary groups. The district has been often victimised by cross-border criminal groups, also with respect to property crime (Bruggeman et al., 1991; Vermeulen et al., 2003). In the fight against these groups, a distinction is often made between regions where these groups commit their crimes (target regions) and regions where they start their operations (Balthau, 2006). Given their large range, these regions mostly differ. Because of the rural nature of this district, it is a typical example of a target region.

The same applies largely to the second district. Situated close to the Dutch border, both Eastern European and border-crossing groups are largely active, although one has to take into account that border-crossing itself is also a method that is often used by Eastern European criminal groups. Hence, the distinction between them is not that strict (Spapens & Fijnaut, 2005, p. 83; Van der Laan & Weenink, 2005, p. 13).

The third region is located in between the three largest Belgian cities, two of them functioning as a main departure node as well. This district is targeted by offenders coming from both cities, but mainly not by border-crossing offender groups. The fourth area is the third largest cities of Belgium. Despite its size, this city mainly functions as a target area and not as a departure node. The city is located near two major motorways, making it an easily accessible target for offenders coming from all over the country.

The second largest Belgian city is chose as the fifth district. This area can be considered as a departure node. Not only does the region suffer from crimes by these groups, the anonymity in certain neighbourhoods provides valuable areas to settle and start criminal operations. Besides the traditional case files, law enforcement agencies haven been working on some proactive cases, trying to gain insight on the less visible background operations of these groups.

Contacting one of the main responsible law enforcement officers in each region, we explained the focus of our research and asked for maximum heterogeneity in the case files. The persons involved supplied us with a number of case files, which they considered as interesting for our research. As such, the set of cases do not represent a random sample.

This approach is far from perfect, as it left our respondents with the possibility to choose which cases they could provide and which not. However, we believe this method has several advantages as well. Within most districts, several people were involved, each one having their own perception of which case being worth studying and which not. As we asked for heterogeneity in the cases, we believe no one better than those people involved in the investigation could evaluate this. They had done the criminal investigation –or knew the one who had– and often knew by heart what formed the particular features of each group. As a direct consequence, we could also obtain some additional background information useful to understand the files to their full extent. Thus, the potential bias of the people involved could be compensated for by the number and variety of districts, the number of persons contacted and the variation asked for.

The result is a data set of 27 case files of so-called 'itinerant crime groups'. In each case, mobility was indeed large. The cases provided information on 49 offenders fulfilling the conditions we used to distinguish 'itinerant crime groups' in the database. Two cases were eliminated from the analysis, one dealing with criminal fencing and therefore providing only indirect information on serious property crimes, the other concerning a case, first believed to be an 'itinerant crime group' but later turned out to be no group or network at all. Because the focus in case selection was put on heterogeneity and not on representativeness, only qualitative conclusions can be drawn and no quantitative statements are made. However, even without the possibility to quantify the results, relevant information can be provided and we obtained a sufficient degree of saturation (Bachman & Schutt, 2008, p. 193; Kleemans, Korf, & Staring, 2008, pp. 328-329).

2.2.3 Offender interviews

The third data source comprises a number of interviews with incarcerated offenders. This data is gathered in two stages. At first, ten offenders are interviewed in the framework of a project commissioned by the Belgian Federal Police. These people functioned as key figures in selling stolen goods. This project aimed at uncovering the fencing networks of itinerant crime groups. As such, the perpetrators were not selected for their knowledge on theft but for the information about criminal fencing networks. Nevertheless, two of them were willing to discuss their involvement in stealing property as well. Additionally, another nineteen offenders are interviewed with respect to theft, bringing the total number of thieves at twenty-one.

Given the main involvement perpetrators from Romania and former Yugoslavia and taking into account the link between mobility and nationality we empirically established, respondents from both nationalities were interviewed. With approval of the Judicial authorities, the principle provided a list of potential respondents, after which some additional required information was obtained: whether the offenders were still incarcerated after a conviction, in which prison and they were willing to cooperate with the researcher. All three issues created a considerable drop-out. Although the data were retrieved from the official sources, some offenders had already been released for several months. Others were in prison because of new offences (of which they were suspected but not yet convicted for) or refused to cooperate.

In the first stage, both Yugoslav en Romanian offenders were interviewed. As the interviews took place with a interpreter, we opted for more uniformity and a focus on Romanian offenders in the second stage. It is particularly these second stage interviews that are dealt with here.

From the Prison Department of the Ministry of Justice, we obtained a list of 67 Romanian offenders who were convicted for property crimes and locked up in one of Belgium's prisons. We contacted 24 of these offender who were willing to participate in our research. Two interviews provided little to no information and a third offender appeared to be in prison for other offences: not property crime, but trafficking human beings. Thus, 21 Romanian thieves were interviewed. Although the sample size only allows an exploratory analysis, the number of offenders has largely been in line with other, similar researches (Cromwell et al., 1991; Polisenska, 2008; Vogel, 1991; Wright & Logie, 1988). Procedural and temporal aspects hampered a real triangulation of the results, but the information retrieved during the interviews was compared with another case file analysis of similar offenders.

The offenders were interviewed in prison. If the respondents agreed, the interviews were tape-recorded. If not – which was the case for six offenders – notes were taken. We explained how the interview would be structured and deliberately stated that we would ask about criminal behaviour and patterns (Yow, 2005). We also stressed the fact that they could withdraw their willingness to participate (Legard, Keegan, & Ward, 2003; Silverman, 2001) or refuse to answer certain questions, in this way reducing the incentive to lie.

Most offenders were suspicious at first, but as the interviews developed they often became more talkative. Several respondents told us afterwards they were glad to be able to tell their own story to someone who really listened was not just after a confession. Due to language issues, all interviews were conducted using an interpreter, his role being twofold. On the one hand, this gave offenders the opportunity to express themselves in their own language, being able to give subtle distinctions. Yet, such a method has a drawback too. Not only is the conversation more artificial because of its indirect nature and intermediate role of the interpreter. This artificial nature also hampers the researcher to take up in the middle of some answers and give the conversation and the various aspects that were dealt with a more natural flow.

The interviews took about one to one and a half hours and followed a semi-structured template. We started with some general questions on personal characteristics, their trip to and stay in Belgium and length of their time in prison. Afterwards, we asked them about their criminal behaviour. Number and type of crimes, planning, movement patterns, target choice and awareness space were addressed. We did not literally ask how many kilometres they had travelled, but whether they offended in the neighbourhood where they stayed and in which regions and municipalities they operated. Finally, we briefly asked them about their experience in prison and gave them the opportunity to add anything they wanted to share and considered relevant but had not been able to tell us yet.

The specificity and size of our sample do not allow to draw general conclusions on offending behaviour. However, previous research in offending patterns has shown that much variation is hidden when only aggregated and general patterns are studied (Smith et al., 2009). Focusing on offenders that have only recently developed certain routines or even have no routines at all in the area where they stay and who travel further than others during their criminal activity allows us to study not the most common offending patterns. As such, we can pay more attention to crime travelling and the concept of awareness space without having to deal with concepts that are otherwise closely related to this spatial awareness, such as distance decay and daily routines. Furthermore, one should not forget this is only one of the used methods. As such, the interviews mainly contribute to a better understanding of certain patterns that are observed in one of the other methods. Finally, being the only method not using official crime-related data, the interviews shed light on more general issues, such as the motivation for travelling and the background of the respondents.

Chapter 3. Itinerant crime groups and travelled distances[1]

In this chapter, we kick-off the empirical section of the study and do so by briefly exploring the empirical study of nationality and mobility in relation to property crimes. Official crime data provide information about the operation of the law enforcement agencies and not exclusively crime itself. In practice, police forces tend to focus on Eastern European offenders when dealing with property crime. If one searches for these offenders, one finds them, as one could also search and find any other nationality of offenders. Hence, this chapter aims at investigating whether or not this search can be empirically justified. If these offenders indeed are more likely to be co-offenders and multiple offenders, this may account for the higher focus on these criminals. Policy documents concerning these groups refer to a high mobility as well. Not being a criminal element as such either, we also study the relation between mobility on the one hand and co-offending and multiple offending on the other.

3.1 Nationality

At first, a general overview was considered. Multiple offending and co-offending are hereby studied. The results according to our distinguished groups of nationalities are presented in Table 3.1.

Table 3.1: Nationality and criminal figures

% nationalities in sample	All	Multiple offending	Co-offending	Multiple & Co-offending
Belgian	67.1	69.9	67.6	69.8
Eastern European	11.3	17.2	12.9	17.9
Other	21.5	12.9	19.5	12.3

[1] A preliminary and shortened version of this chapter has been published as: Van Daele, S. (2008). Organised property crimes in Belgium: the case of the 'itinerant crime groups'. Global Crime, 9(3), 241-247.

This appears to indicate that offenders of different nationalities commit a different number of crimes, as confirmed in Table 3.2. This is confirmed by a one-way ANOVA ($F(2;64406) = 51.57$; $p<.001$). One can conclude, therefore, that Eastern European offenders commit more offences on average than offenders with a different nationality.

Table 3.2: Average numbers for each group

	Average number of offences	Average number of offenders
Belgian	2.2	2.3
Eastern European	2.8	2.7
Other	1.8	2.2

The next stage was to link co-offending to nationality. As co-offending is a crime characteristic and nationality an offender characteristic, this can be assessed in several ways. We chose to recode the data to keep the offenders as counting units. Hence, for each offender, the average number of co-offenders per crime is calculated. Eastern European offenders committed their crimes on average with 2.7 other people, compared with 2.3 for the Belgian offenders and 2.2 for 'the rest'. A one-way ANOVA shows that these differences are statistically significant ($F(2;64406) = 235.32$; $p<.001$). Afterwards, the percentage of co-offenders are analysed. This includes all offenders of which the average number of perpetrators was higher than 1, meaning they have committed at least one crime together with another criminal. These proportions are quite similar with those of the general sample and indicate that 67.6% of co-offending criminals are Belgian, 12.9% have an Eastern European nationality and 19.5% belong to the 'rest' group.

In terms of the numbers of criminals who both multiply offend and co-offend, the nationality structure is fairly similar to that of all multiple offenders: the percentage of offenders who are Eastern European amounts to 17.9 per cent, compared with 69.8 per cent who are Belgian offenders and 12.3 per cent who make up 'the rest'. These proportions are statistically significant from what we might expect ($Chi^2 = 137.9$; $df = 2$; $p<.001$).

Based on our data, nationality provides an indication of multiple offending. Of course, this should not lead to certain groups in the population being stigmatised. It also does not negate the presence of organised crime within Eastern European countries themselves (Hignett, 2004), or the export of Western organised crime to Eastern Europe (Siegel, 2006). It simply indicates the existence of

Eastern European gangs who are involved in organised property crimes in Western Europe, in this case Belgium.

3.2 Mobility

The next characteristic to be studied in this phase of the research was mobility, or the distance between a criminal's residence and the location of their offence. In order to minimise errors, the real – observed – residence was preferred over the officially registered residence. The residence of only about half the offenders (N=31068) was known. For offenders residing outside Belgium, only the country of residence was mentioned; as more precise information was missing, these were filtered out, leaving a sample of 28907 offenders. Thus, 93% of the offenders do reside in Belgium.

The average distance per offender was 14.6km. This is considerably greater than that given in literature, which indicates averages of less than 7km (Capone & Nichols, 1976; Edwards & Grace, 2006; Phillips, 1980; White, 1932). Co-offending criminals tend to travel slightly further than others (15.0km, compared with 13.8km for sole-offending criminals). The average distance for multiple offenders increases further to 21.4km, which is significantly higher than the 14.3km found for offenders who are recorded fewer than ten times ($t = 8.018$; $df = 1082.1$; $p<.001$).

Criminals who both multiply offended and co-offended travel on average 21.4km to commit their crimes, compared with a distance of only 14.3km for the remaining criminals ($t = 7.812$; $df = 997.1$; $p<.001$). Hence, multiple, co-offending criminals travel further than others, indicating that mobility is a suitable indicator of criminality against property.

3.3 Itinerant crime groups

Based on our data both nationality and mobility were clear indicators of organised property crimes. Two additional factors can be tested. First, by combining mobility and nationality it was found that Eastern European multiple co-offenders travelled on average 37.4km, compared with only 18.4km for Belgian offenders and 23.5km for 'the rest' ($F(2;941) = 27.2$; $p<.001$). Linking nationality and offences committed further than 30km (as can been defined as 'long distances')(Laukkanen & Santtila, 2006) from the residence (N=227), we noticed that the proportion of Eastern European offenders rose to 30.8 per cent, compared with 58.1 per cent of the Belgian and 11.0 per cent of the other offenders ($Chi^2 = 84.0$; $df = 2$; $p<.001$). Hence, mobility and nationality appear to correlate. Second, it could be argued that the data is biased because the authorities deliberately search for particular types of criminal, potentially creating an overrepresentation of mobile and Eastern European people.

It is necessary to explore the link between the criminal, the crime and the date it was committed to establish whether this is the case. Due to the level of abstraction, the counting unit in this comparison cannot be used for other comparisons. However, it is the best way to illustrate this particular issue.

The fight against this particular crime phenomenon was only embedded in policy since 2004. The 2002 and 2003 data indicate that the above findings were already present at that time. The proportion of offenders who were Eastern European was similar for both periods (10.6 per cent in the period 2002-2003, compared with 10.0 per cent since 2004). Other factors show a similarity in occurrence in the two periods – the number of offences committed by East European offenders (respectively 24.7 and 25.5), the number of offenders (2.8 for both periods) and the distance they travelled (respectively 34.8km and 32.7km). These data differ from the above described percentages due to the use of other counting units. Nevertheless, the results indicate that the data collected post-2004 is not the result of authorities targeting this particular group.

Policy formulated on the basis of non-criminal characteristics such as nationality and mobility runs the risk of creating self-fulfilling prophecies if the authorities focus their attention on people who possess these characteristics. It also risks creating a criminal policy based on the stigmatising of particular groups. It is therefore important to study the empirical basis behind new policies.

This chapter has taken a first look at the so-called itinerant crime groups to explore the empirical basis of their existence. Although the phenomenon was initially only perceived in a limited number of criminal cases, nevertheless this chapter's analysis of the defining characteristics of this group – both criminal and non-criminal – indicates that multiple and co-offenders are more likely to travel longer distances. Among these subjects Eastern European offenders are overrepresented. Of course, the majority is still comprised of Belgians, but the increase of the Eastern European perpetrators is striking. Such an approach produces a picture of the make-up of this criminal group, although it does not say anything about the causes of this criminal phenomenon. The argument as to whether the figures are the result of a greater focus on people with these characteristics can be countered by the similarity in findings before and after this phenomenon was identified. Thus, the non-criminal features do not determine whether or not one is criminal, but rather indicate that criminals often have these characteristics. We do not suggest that by proving the existence of itinerant Eastern European crime groups the case is solved. On the contrary, some new criminological challenges are born, such as why these groups travel such distances to commit crimes (Ponsaers, 2004) and how they can best be combated. These challenges can now be taken up.

Chapter 4. Distance decay and itinerant crime groups[2]

Traditional criminological research on journey-to-crime has found that most offenders operate on a local level. The reasons for this can be found in routine activities (Cohen & Felson, 1979), awareness space (Brantingham & Brantingham, 1981b) and rational choice (Cornish & Clarke, 1986b). Because criminal operations tend to be oriented locally, police authorities can be organized locally, with broader data sharing and police operations only occurring in extraordinary cases or for particular crime types (Bowling & Foster, 2002; Newburn, 2008, p. 232; Virta, 2002; Yarwood, 2007).

In the present chapter, we want to address to what extent these groups are more mobile. Are they just more mobile as we demonstrated in the previous chapter, or also mobile to a different extent? Additionally, we attempt to examine where they operate more precisely. In this way, we want to focus on patterns of these groups, compared with other offenders, and what the implications are for police authorities.

We find that their mobility challenges some common principles of police management and organization. Mobile criminals create a need for police forces to cooperate, share their knowledge and conduct joint investigations. The fact that this now occurs for rather "ordinary" property crimes may cause a shift in the organization of police activities.

Each main variable of definition is considered: group offending, systematic/multiple offending, and Eastern European origin. We also added another one: operating from outside Belgium or from one of Belgium's main cities. We do so because of two elements. First, albeit not crucial, this is mentioned in the definition too. Second, we believe the place where criminals depart may be relevant for their offending patterns, making it interesting to consider

To compare crime patterns, the data sample is divided into several categories. Afterwards average distances and distance decay patterns for the various

[2] This chapter has been inspired by:
Van Daele, S., & Vander Beken, T. (2010). Journey to crime of 'itinerant crime groups'. Policing - An International Journal of Police Strategies & Management, 33(2), 339-353.

groups are established. As outlined above, in order to facilitate comparisons between the various groups, the distances were simplified by using categories of 10km each. This enabled particular groups to be compared more easily.

4.1 Sample groups

Before dividing the sample up into specific groups, some information on the whole sample of offender-offence combinations is drawn out. The average distance – between home (Rengert, 2004, pp. 169-170) and offence location – covered to commit a serious property offence in Belgium (N=67981) is about 19.1km. This is considerably higher than most literature indicates. It is likely to be caused by the nature of our data, which are gathered nationwide, whereas most journey-to-crime studies only take into account crime trips within one city. Including crime trips that begin in Sheffield and end outside the city, Wiles and Costello (2000, p. 16) also observed longer distances of 6.8 miles (10.9km) on average, compared with only 1.9 (3.0km) miles for crime trips within Sheffield. Furthermore, it is also higher than the results we presented in the previous chapter. This is related to the fact that we now use offender-offence combinations, while we used the offender as unit of analysis in the previous chapter. Other research has indicated that travelled distances increase as an offender has committed more offences (Barker, 2000). Thus, taking into account offender-offence combinations makes us count each distance and, consequently, count multiple offenders several times (once for each offence they have committed), while single offenders – who tend to travel not as far – are only counted once.

Notwithstanding these long average distances, a regular distance decay pattern was observed (figure 4.1). This pattern indicates that 59.5 percent of the serious property crimes were committed within 10km of the offender's home. With increasing distances, the number of offences committed decreased consistently. This swift decline results in only 14.6 percent of crimes being committed between 10–19km away from home, and 7.0 percent between 20–29km.

After the general distance decay pattern had been established, the various features assigned to these groups were considered: co-offending, multiple offending, nationality and type of residential area.

Figure 4.1: General distance decay pattern

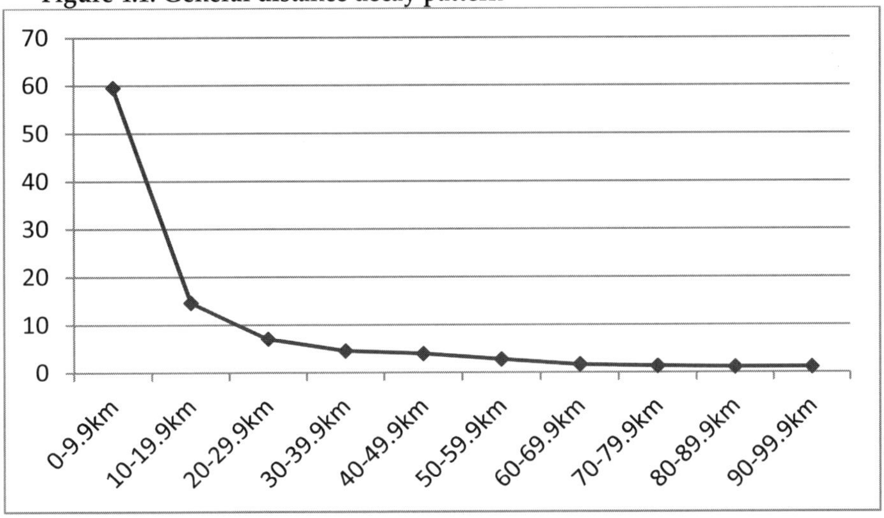

4.2 Co-offending

A first factor involved co-offending. The mean distance for offences committed by two or more people (N=41590) was 20.1km, compared with 17.6km for offences committed by an offender acting alone (N=26391). This very modest difference is to be expected, giving the limited correlation (Pearson's r= .052) between number of offenders and distances travelled. This similarity was also reflected in the distance decay curve of both groups, which was very similar (see figure 4.2).

This can also be found in previous work by Bernasco (2006). He concluded that offenders mostly travelled from the residence of one of the offenders. As the present method calculated one offence by two offenders twice, the second distance will be larger, influencing the result and seeming to indicate more offences being committed further away.

Figure 4.2: Distance decay patterns and co-offending

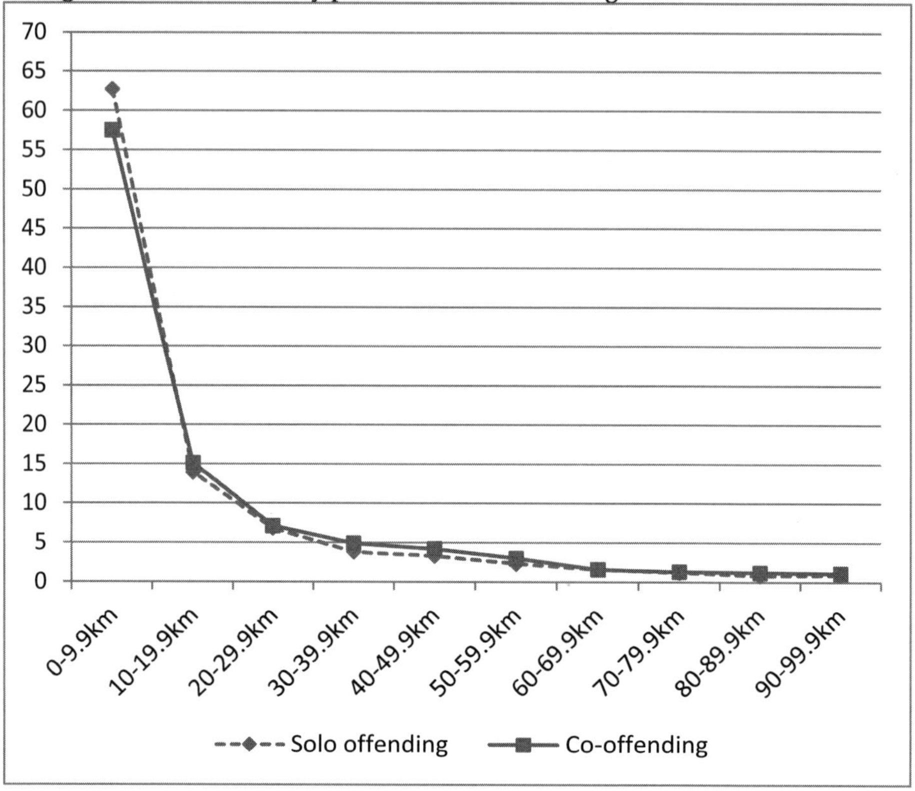

4.3 Multiple offending

In the definition of itinerant crime groups, the targeted offenders are systematically offending, and can be understood as being multiple offenders. Using the method of Elffers (2003) and Ferwerda et al. (1995), those who have committed ten or more offences were classed as "multiple offenders". The mean distance travelled for the crimes committed by multiple offenders (N=19485) in this study was 22.8km, compared with 15.0km for the others (N=48779). This difference is significant at the .01 level. It confirms the link between the number of offences and travelled distances as found by Barker (2000), which is translated in a Pearson's r of .115 in our sample. Whereas Barker concluded that number of offences and distances travelled were only correlated within the first five offences, this was not the case here. Although lower than in total, distance and number of offences were still correlated, even within the group of multiple offenders. (r=.07, $p<.001$) This higher mean distance was also represented in the distance decay pattern (see figure 4.3).

Figure 4.3: Distance decay patterns and multiple offending

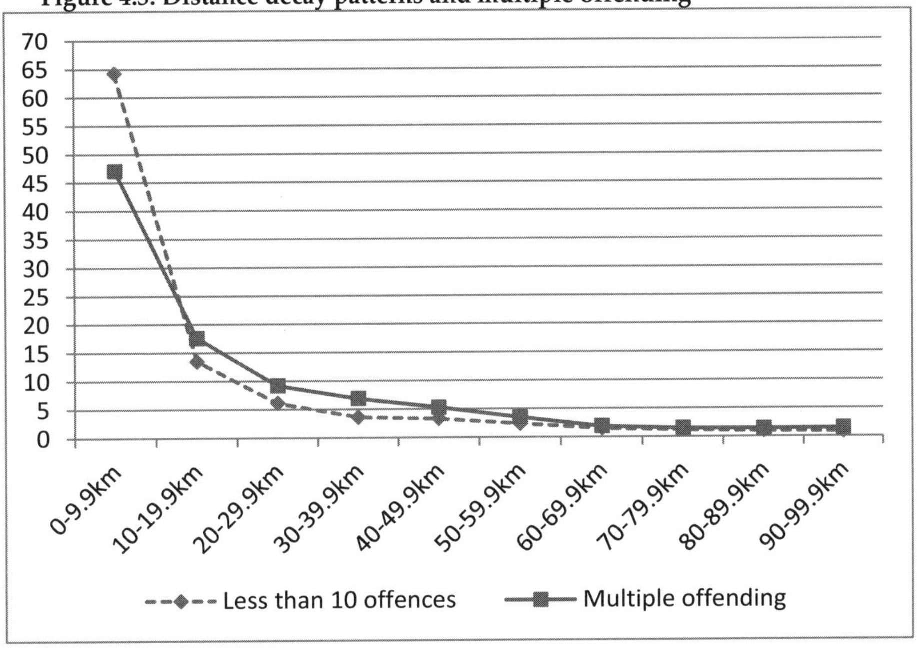

Multiple offenders committed their crimes further away from home more often than other offenders. Only 47.1 percent of the offences they commit were carried out within 10km of where they lived, compared with 64.2 percent for the other offenders. Nevertheless, this difference does not have an implication for the existence of the classical distance decay pattern for both groups. Thus, multiple offenders travelled further than other offenders, but this does not imply they filter out their immediate awareness space.

4.4 Nationality of offenders

A final offender characteristic that the data set enabled us to investigate is nationality. The first group was made up of criminals with Eastern European nationality (N=7078). This group was chosen because of specific criminal activity that has occurred in recent years. Since the turn of the century a number of Western European countries (including Belgium, France, the Netherlands, and Germany) have recorded an increase in the involvement of Eastern European criminal gangs in property crimes (De Ruyver, 2006: 5; Spapens and Fijnaut, 2005: 83–85; Korps Landelijke Politiediensten, 2004: 87; Van der Laan and Weenink, 2005). Due to the high level of interest in these particular offenders, who commit a considerable amount of property crimes in Belgium—25 percent is often mentioned (De Ruyver, 2006; Ponsaers, 2004)—we chose to identify Eastern European offenders as a separate group. They included nationals from what used to be the Eastern Bloc, including the former Soviet republics and the Soviet satellite states, but also including the countries that were covered by the Federal Republic of Yugoslavia and Albania. The second group contained all Belgian offenders (N=51383) and a third group contained all offenders from other nationalities (N=9518).

The average distances travelled were 34.7km for Eastern European offenders, 17.0km for Belgian offenders and 19.2km for the third group. Eastern European offenders apparently tended to travel twice as far as other offenders. The resulting distance decay pattern is shown in figure 4.4. For offences committed by Belgian offenders or the third group, patterns of offences tended to follow the classical distance decay curve. More than 60 percent of offences were committed less than 10km from home, sharply declining afterwards.

Eastern European offenders, however, produced a very different distance decay curve. Only 32.3 percent committed their offences close to home, while 14.7 percent and 9 percent committed offences in the second and third distance categories. The number of offences committed increased again slightly in the fourth and fifth category, after which the proportion remained consistently higher than that of the other groups. For property crimes committed by Eastern European offenders, the establishment of a distance decay pattern is clearly not straightforward. The distance travelled on crime trips among these Eastern European offenders was nearly double that of other offenders. This is also accompanied by a slightly deviating distance decay pattern, which has not yet been observed for the other features.

Another observation has also been made concerning nationality. In our dataset, less than half of the offenders had a registered residence. This percentage was lowest for Eastern European offenders (35.8 percent), compared with Belgian (52.6 percent) and other foreign offenders (41.2 percent). This indicates that residences of Eastern European offenders were more difficult to assess than for other offenders, possibly due to their moving more frequently (Ponsaers, 2004).

Attributing a temporary residence to all crimes in the data would probably cause crime trips to be overestimated. It is quite possible that anchor points (Rengert, 2004) and residence interpretation (Wiles & Costello, 2000) cause such deviations.

Figure 4.4: Distance decay patterns and nationality

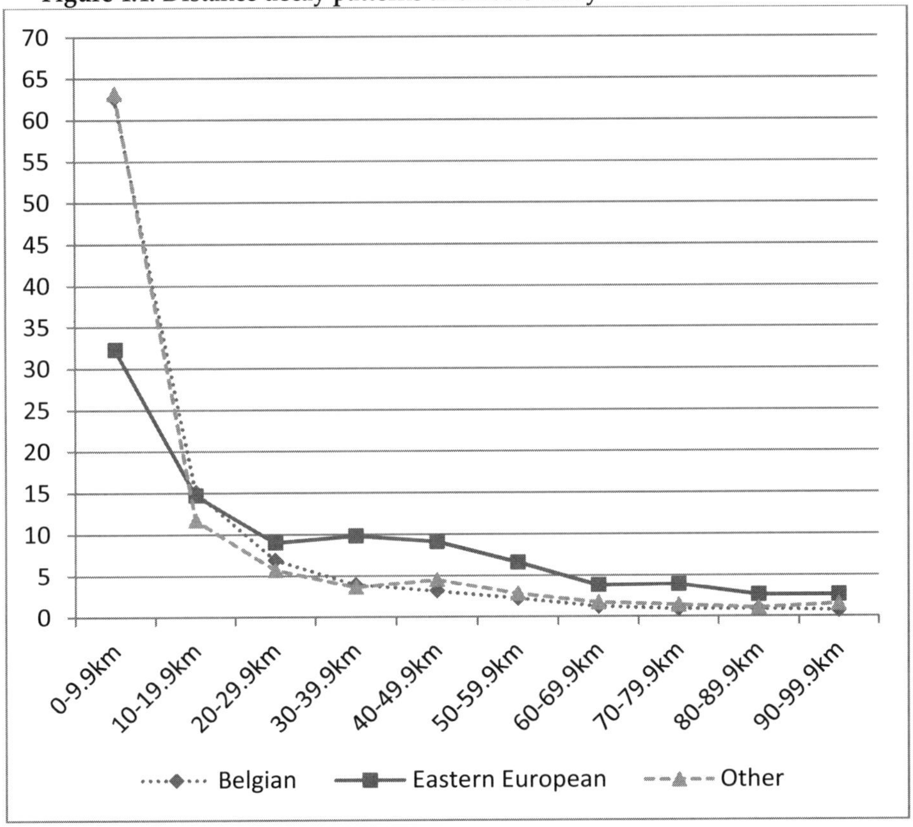

4.5 Residence in an urban or rural setting

We also explored whether living in an urban or rural area was significant in terms of distance travelled to commit an offence. Belgium has seven cities with more than 100,000 inhabitants: Brussels, Antwerp, Ghent, Charleroi, Liege, Bruges and Namur. These were classed as urban areas, while the rest of the country was classed as rural. Distances were studied in relation to where the offender lived. The mean travelled distance for offenders living in one of these seven cities was 14.5km (N= 20882), compared with 21.2km for those living in rural areas (N=47099). This confirms the general premise that urban residents have less need to travel: work, shopping and leisure activities are more likely to take place within a small area, while this is not the case for rural residents. Therefore, we could expect the awareness space (Brantingham & Brantingham, 1981b) – and, therefore, the crime trips size – of offenders living in rural areas to be larger, something that has been found before by Clinard (1944).

Figure 4.5: Distance decay patterns and residence

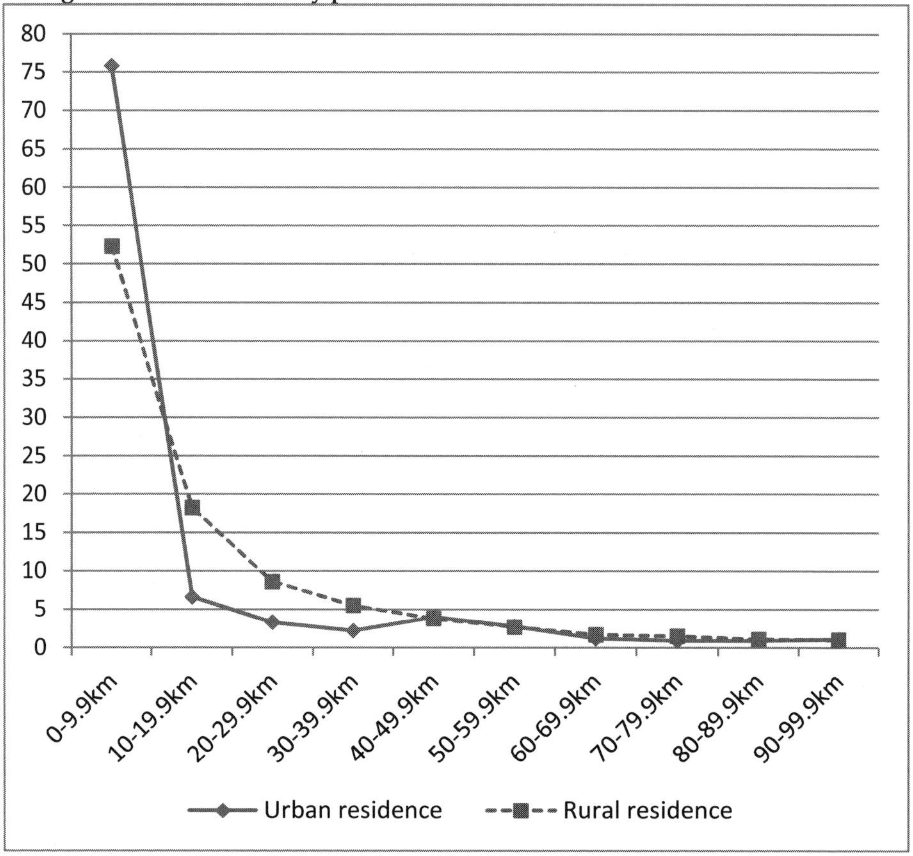

An expected observation is that offenders living in urban areas committed a higher percentage of offences in their immediate environment. This percentage was higher than for those who live in rural areas (75.8 percent vs. 52.3 percent). The number of crimes committed then swiftly declined with distance, and only 6.6 percent of crimes were committed within the second distance band in the case of urban residence, compared with 18.2 percent for those from rural areas at the same distance. However, the second small peak in the fifth band, which accounts for 4 percent of the offences, was unexpected when compared with only 2.2 percent of offences in the fourth. Therefore, although a general distance decay pattern was observed, this pattern tends to deviate slightly for offenders from urban areas.

4.6 Combining the features: itinerant crime groups

The Belgian definition attributes four features to these groups. We have found each feature separately to be related to higher mobility, although only two—nationality and residence—showed slight changes in the distance decay pattern. As a final step, we combined all features and studied the distance decay pattern for these groups (N=2095). The mean travelled distance for itinerant crime groups was 42.8km.

Figure 4.6: Distance decay pattern for itinerant crime groups

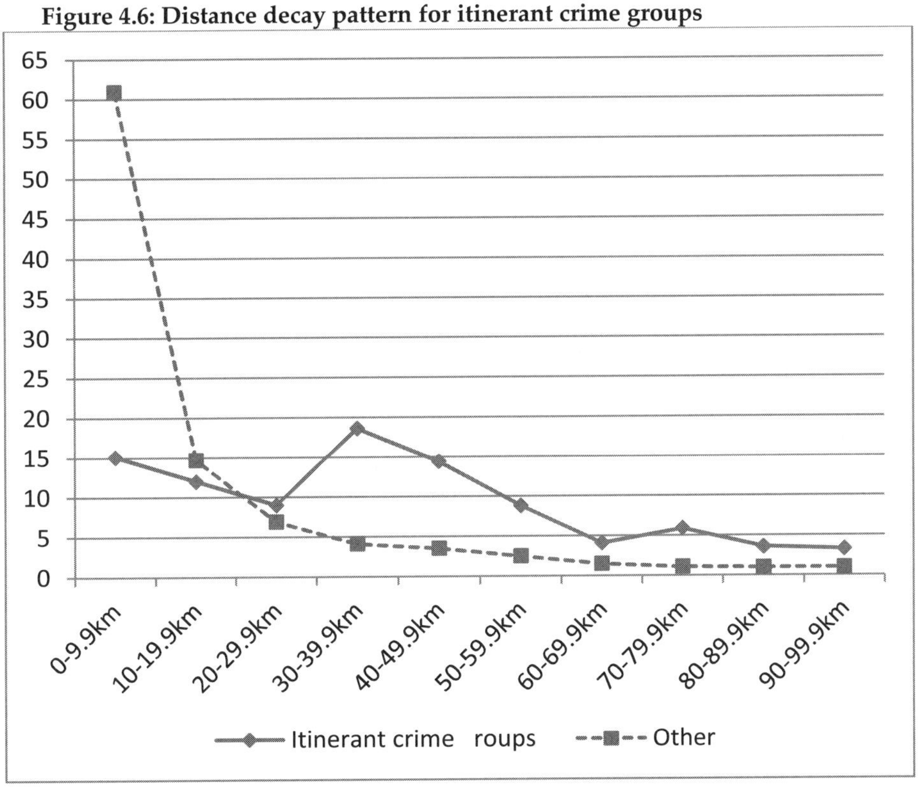

Comparing the distance decay pattern with the generally observed pattern (Figure 4.6), we notice striking differences. For itinerant crime groups, there was not much decay to consider. On the contrary, distances between 30 and 50km were more frequently travelled than distances of less than 10km. Despite the general tendency to stay near home, members of itinerant crime groups appeared to favour targets that were located further away.

Using police data on serious property offences in Belgium, differing crime–residence distances have been identified. For those features of itinerant crime groups identified by policy makers, travelled distances and distance decay patterns were examined.

Each separate characteristic showed longer average distances travelled, but most of these differences did not affect the decay pattern. Small exceptions were distances between 30 and 50km, which appeared slightly overrepresented for Eastern European offenders and criminals living in urban areas. Combining the various features, a serious shift in the decay pattern was observed: the heart of the distance pattern was moved from crimes at less than 10km from home to offences committed at over 30km away from home.

This confirms what Rengert al. (1999) suggest, that distance decay patterns may vary between offender groups. A general representation of distance decay may conceal a lot of information. A simple division of offenders into some easily identified groups revealed substantial differences in distances travelled, and even differing distance decay patterns. We do not, in this chapter, analyze our findings at the individual level. Thus, we do not attribute the distance decay pattern to some sort of ecological fallacy. We would put it even more strongly: distance decay variations and deviations do not only occur at the individual level. Even on an aggregated level, with a limited number of distinctions, variations and deviations appear. Unfortunately, these differences become invisible when the general distance decay pattern is observed.

This observation provides a theoretical framework for further study and analysis of distance decay patterns. A second step is how these differences can be interpreted, particularly in relation to the phenomenon of itinerant crime groups. The varying distance decay patterns can be explained using three approaches: Target-oriented and offender-oriented approaches, which are the most common, and a route-oriented approach.

The first approach is target-oriented. Cohen and Felson (1979), in their routine activity approach, developed the idea that changing life-patterns influenced the rise in crime in the 1960s. As crime requires a convergence in time and space of likely offenders, suitable guardians and the absence of capable guardians, the change in routine activities within the eventual victims' population dispelled the presence of capable guardians. Those routine activities are all recurrent and prevalent activities that provide for basic population and individual needs (Cohen & Felson, 1979, p. 593). Cohen and Felson highlighted in particular the shift from routine activities at home to elsewhere, leaving residences unattended for longer periods. In relation to robberies, research by Groff (2007) strongly supports this, concluding that crime will increase as the amount of time spent away from home rises. In a recent poll, Belgian people appeared to commute longer and further than the European average (J.I.R., 2009; Stepstone Survey, 2009). Because Belgian people are willing to commute longer, they will more often stay in rural areas, although they work in one of the main cities. One could therefore argue that the amount of time spent away from home is higher in residential areas that are situated between 30km and 50km from the main cities. This can be seen as a macro-level approach.

As such, a routine activities approach could partly account for the longer distances and the fact that targeting rural areas could be successful. Target-oriented differences may explain a proportion of these patterns. Yet, they cannot account for the differences between various offender types. After all, the targets are the same for all offenders. Whether they decide to stay around the larger cities or to travel to rural areas depends on the individual target perception and appreciation, not on the targets themselves. If two offenders head out for a search, starting from the same city, there are no objective target-related reasons why offender A will look near home and offender B will travel further or vice versa.

A second group of explanations is offender-oriented. Important characteristics in this perspective are age, experience and ethnicity. The least mobile offenders are young and inexperienced, and belong to visible minority groups (Gabor & Gottheil, 1984, p. 270). Due to this last feature, we distinguished three instead of two groups of nationalities. Alongside the group of Eastern European offenders, we distinguished Belgian from foreign offenders, as the latter belong to a minority. We measured experienced by comparing the number of offences committed, as Barker (2000) indicates that distances will increase with the number of offences committed.

Eastern European offenders committed more offences on average and, thus, are more experienced. They were also older than Belgian offenders: Their average year of birth was 1976, compared to 1978 for the Belgian offenders and 1974 for the "other" group. According to the analysis of variances, these differences are significant at the .01 level. This may explain why Eastern European offenders travel further than Belgian offenders. However, this does not explain why the distances travelled by the third group are shorter. Finally, visible differences in ethnicity can explain variations in mobility (De Poot et al., 2005; Gabor & Gottheil, 1984, p. 270). Although Eastern Europeans have a different nationality to the country in which they are living, their ethnicity often does not visibly differ from Belgian offenders and therefore their mobility is less restricted than might be expected for foreign offenders.

These explanations possibly account for some of the longer average distances travelled. Yet, they do not explain the generation of a second peak between 30–49.9km. A third explanation is therefore necessary, and this can be considered route-oriented. Elffers (2004, pp. 184-186) discusses the effect of so-called barriers that create higher cost increases on short distances. These might be waterways, inaccessible terrains, and so on. However, routes can also function as facilitators for travelling further. In our sample, most offences were committed in the area where the offender lived. Other popular target areas were those easily accessed by using the network of Belgian highways. It appears that urban areas not only increase nearby crime opportunities, they also make it easier for offenders to travel further. Of course, the question remains why this is different for Eastern European offenders compared to others. Ponsaers (2004) suggested that the so-called "itinerant crime groups" conflict with prevailing criminological theories. This assumption is, perhaps, a step too far. Nevertheless, it would benefit from further research on personal motivations for travelling. The offender-oriented explanations should therefore be further opened up to other characteristics and personal issues, such as motivation, lifestyle, habits and perception. Further elaborating these features could, in combination with an understanding of the evolutions in the environment, help us to better understand the method of these groups and take up the current and upcoming challenges (Verfaillie & Vander Beken, 2008).

From a theoretical perspective, these findings indicate that distance decay patterns do very between rather basic groups distinctions. The observation of this pattern is important from a policy perspective as well. Rattner and Portnov (2007) distinguished crime-exporting from crime-importing regions. Considering each feature separately, an overall focus on local offenders is still in place, despite the differences between various types of offenders. When we combined these features and, thus, discussed so-called itinerant crime groups, another picture appeared.

Although itinerant crime groups mainly operate from large cities that do provide plenty of crime opportunities, they opt to travel further and mainly target places at 30–50km from their residence. These groups do not initiate their crimes in crime-exporting regions. On the contrary, they start in areas that provide plenty of criminal opportunities. Nevertheless, these groups do export crime to other areas. As such, their methods pose new challenges to law enforcement authorities. Due to the concentration of people and criminal opportunities, police resource management has mostly focused on urban areas. However, these groups tend to commit their crimes at greater distances from home. Given that the main Belgian cities are located about 50–60km from each other, these groups target those areas that are located between the cities. This creates more work for police forces in rural areas. Moreover, rural police forces cannot fight these groups by themselves, as the gangs operate across a number of regions, and therefore each police force only knows about some of their crimes. As a consequence, rural police forces need to cooperate in order to achieve maximum results. They also need to cooperate with teams from urban areas, as the latter can provide information on where these groups reside. Such strategies have been widely adopted in Belgium, under coordination of the Federal Prosecutor (Balthau, 2006; FOD Justitie et al., 2007). In other countries where this phenomenon has been observed (Van Geffen, 2009), the approach is less coordinated and more related to individual cases. Given the growing awareness of the phenomenon of Eastern European property crime gangs, most countries could well benefit from a more comprehensive framework within which these groups can be combated. After all, these groups do pose challenges to criminology, both from a theoretical perspective and from a police management and police priorities perspective.

Chapter 5. Heterogeneity of itinerant crime groups[3]

Next to the empirical observation of the offenders' mobility, we further explore the various characteristics of these groups. In this way, we aim to determine some features that contribute to the higher mobility and help us understand the underlying mechanisms of these criminals' operation. In decoupling the study of these groups from their mobility, we extend our general perception of their methods and organisation. Due to the selection mechanism used in our analysis, a large variety of crime groups are captured.

5.1 Levels of organisation and structure

One of the issues in which this is easily observed is the organisational structure of these groups. The Belgian annual report on organised crime (Dienst voor het Strafrechtelijk Beleid, 2005, pp. 32-34; 2007, pp. 62-64) distinguished four levels of organisation, ranging from highly structured and internationally active to opportunistic, temporary active groups. The highly organised groups can be dealt with as criminal organisations, but for the small groups, this is less likely. Our analysis found both highly structured as well as barely structured groups, including those in between.

At one extreme, we studied a highly structured organisation of Georgian origin. The group was known mainly for the organisation of vehicle thefts and contained various organisational levels. There was a leader, residing in Belgium and living in great luxury. He had some people he trusted and worked closely together with. Other people were situated a bit lower in the hierarchy: couriers, a forger and several people involved in the maintenance of the 'obchak' – a word used to describe the system of social and financial security within Russian-like criminal organisations (Lyman & Potter, 1997). At the lowest level were the executioners of the crimes. They had a much less luxurious lifestyle and were sometimes 'transferred' from this gang to other gangs abroad.

---

[3] Some of the concepts in this paper have been published as:
Van Daele, S., & Vander Beken, T. (2010). Exploring itinerant crime groups. European Journal on Criminal Policy and Research, 16(1), 1-13.

At the other extreme, we found a group, coming over to Belgium for a short period. Offenders stayed with a Belgian couple and operated in small groups. There was no real structure or leadership and the offenders lived in poor circumstances.

Structural features of most groups are situated somewhere between the two cases described above. However, we chose not to further divide into categories. Structural features are to be viewed as a continuum: we established the two extremes and observed various types in between. Therefore, any further division would be artificial and influenced by personal choice and interpretation. Moreover, defining the structural typology of a group is not always straightforward. Depending on the attention paid by investigating officers, groups can seem to be much more or less structured. We encountered one group which was loosely structured according to the case file and our police contact. However, other features such as violence, number of offences and group size resemble that of more structured groups. Instead of further dividing the groups, we see more added value in linking group structure to other features like offender characteristics, crime types, mobility, strategies and the criminal fence.

Group sizes differ as well. Group size is not always linked to organisational levels. Of course, highly structured groups will have more than two or three offenders. In general, hierarchically structured groups are larger. Yet, some groups consist of several offenders – 15 for example – outside a clearly defined structure. In these cases, opportunistic and temporary cooperation leads to more offenders being involved.

5.2 Offender characteristics

The vast majority of offenders are men. They are involved in criminal operations and in case of hierarchy, men have the highest functions. This does not mean that no women are involved. In about half of the groups studied, some women play a role within the organization as well. Most of them are partners of one of the male offenders. They are active in supporting activities like providing accommodation, logistic support and sometimes even fencing. It is not always clear to what extent their contributions are essential to the group activities. When residing with their respective partners, it is not astonishing that their cell phone numbers are encountered during the investigation. Thus, their activities, be it essential or not, are likely to be revealed as well. Despite the generally limited involvement of women, two cases reveal otherwise. In these two cases, women are active in the group's criminal operations and not only provide support.

Most offenders are rather young or middle-aged. Several groups contain offenders born in the 1950s or even the 1940s. A slightly larger proportion is born in the 1960s. The vast majority of nearly all offender groups are perpetrators born in the 1970s and the first half of the 1980s. Most offenders are in their twenties or thirties. Several groups contain older offenders as well. Most offenders are experienced too. They often have a criminal record, either in their home country, Belgium or even a third country. The crimes they have been known for mostly include property crimes, but also violence – whether or not while committing property crimes – fraud, forgery and sometimes even drug crimes. While most offenders are adults and often experienced, this is not always the case. Two groups use minors for criminal purposes. Remarkable is the fact that these are the same groups involving women for crime and not only for supporting activities. They each comprise several families and within these families, crime is a common activity, not only committed by men, but also by other family members such as women and children, so it appears. This does not mean that the methods are the same: women and children mostly commit their crimes by using deception or tricks. They sometimes try to gain access to target premises by pretending to sell certain items. Other methods include ringing the doorbell to see whether there is any presence. If someone opens the door, they ask for simple things – the road to a nearby village for example – and if not, they burgle the house.

As mentioned, some groups consist of family members, which immediately explains their origin and the relationship between the offenders. Yet, this does not mean that all offenders within these groups are family. There are mostly a number of families, surrounded by other individuals. This results in a mix between families and other. We believe it is therefore better to speak of clan-wise structure instead of family structure. This clan structure is observed in most gypsy groups. Some of them have come to Western Europe more recently, while others have stayed here for longer periods and have mixed with indigenous groups. While the first are active throughout the country, the latter are mostly active in the border regions.

Not all groups are characterized by a clan structure. Within some groups, the members mention no previous relationship at all. Their cases show no evidence of other relationships than having come to Belgium separately, in search for a better life, and having met each other by coincidence. In search for work, they made contact with people in the same situation and in this way, got involved in crime. Yet, this is not the case for all groups. In several cases, offenders originated from the same region or even the same town. Although it is not always explicitly mentioned in the files – being no investigation priority – it is quite likely that they have known each other beforehand.

Members of other groups seem to have no known personal relationship, but are accepted in a certain group because they are part of the broader structure within which the group operates. This is particularly observed in highly structured groups.

A final offender characteristic is nationality. It is often mentioned that these groups are from Eastern European origin. That does not mean that only Eastern European offenders systematically commit property crimes. Some groups contain a mix of nationalities, within or outside Eastern Europe. It mostly occurred that there is one dominant nationality, surrounded and supported by several figures of other nationalities. The encountered main nationalities are Romanian – with or without Moldovan – and former Yugoslavian (each 8 cases), Albanian and Georgian (each 3 cases) and Polish (1 case). Some districts consider other nationalities as well. Two groups are mainly French, one group Dutch and one Belgian. Border district police forces have observed groups with similar methods but not of Eastern European origin. Thus, they do not consider Eastern European nationality as a necessary condition for itinerant crime groups. Several groups have no homogenous composition. Surrounding people have nationalities ranging from all sorts of Eastern European nationalities (those already mentioned above, but also offenders originating from Ukraine, Bulgaria, Slovenia, Russia, Czech Republic, Belarus) to Western European offenders (French, Dutch, Belgian and naturalized Belgian) and even Southern European (Italian) and Northern African (Moroccan) offenders.

Observing only offender features, it already appears that 'itinerant crime group' is a heterogeneous concept. The majority of offenders are men, young adults or middle-aged, of Eastern European nationalities. However, they are supported by older offenders, women and offenders from other nationalities. In some cases, other offenders' activities extend support: in some gypsy groups, women play an active role in criminal behaviour, and so do even children. In other groups, involved in border region crime, Eastern European nationalities are not as dominant as elsewhere.

5.3 Crime types

Itinerant crime groups are mainly active in the area of property crimes. The number of offences ranges from four to more than 400. These are only estimates, as it is not always possible to prove the involvement of a group into a certain crime. Therefore, enforcement authorities sometimes choose to focus more on investigating and proving a rather limited number of crimes than bringing all highly likely group activities in picture. There is no clear correlation between the number of crimes committed and the duration of activity: some groups have been active for more than two years and have 'only' committed about 80 property crimes, others have succeeded in committing probably up to 400 crimes just in eight months, of which they were really active for less than five. There is some link between group structure and number of crimes. Yet, this should not be overrated. Well-structured groups particularly choosing their targets and specialized in certain crimes will very likely commit less crimes than small groups committing random burglaries.

Home burglaries and car thefts occur most often and are committed by almost any group. Other crimes are committed by some groups. An alternative to car thefts is stealing anything inside the vehicle: electronic devices but also work material that is locked in vans. Commercial burglaries require more knowledge and are committed less often. Nevertheless, a couple of groups are specialized in it, but they mostly commit fewer crimes within a certain period. The same counts for metal thefts and thefts of documents: it is not an activity in which most groups engage, but the domain of a few groups. Even more specialization is required for skimming. Thus, the latter has only been observed in a minority of groups.

Ram raiding is the final property crime type encountered in our case file analysis. Although few groups tend to commit a limited amount of ram raids, two groups make it their main criminal activity. Both of them belong to the 'border region crime' type described above: the offenders are not illegally residing Eastern Europeans, but Western European, operating at both sides of the border.

It is typical for these groups that they are active in the area of 'ordinary' property crimes. However, one police officer told us that this had more to do with the police structure in Belgium – each police department being divided according to crime types they investigate – than with the activities of these groups. Because the cases were provided by the property crime departments of the police, we had only limited information on other crimes than property offences. Yet, there was often information on other crimes these groups were involved in. We did not consider criminal fence as a separate crime type, because it is a consequence of committed property crimes. Still, ten case files dealt with multi-criminal groups. This does not mean that the rest is not involved in other crimes than property offences. It only means that there was no such information obtained from the case file.

Five groups have been known for forging identification papers. By using fake identity papers, offenders succeed in moving more freely into and throughout Europe. In this way, the use of false papers is not completely strange. Other crimes have different degrees of seriousness ranging from prohibited use of weapons and use of violence (one case each) to severe crimes such as manslaughter (three cases) and more internationally oriented crimes like trafficking in human beings (one case) and drug trafficking (seven cases). Multi-criminality is linked to structural features. Two multi-crime groups have only limited structures. However, their multi-criminal behaviour is limited to forgery, prohibited use of weapons and drug-related activities. Most groups known for multi-criminal activity, however, are well-structured, have international links and/or operate on an international level.

Itinerant crime groups are known for systematically committing property crimes. These range from rather easily approachable examples, such as burglary and car theft, to more specialized offences like metal theft, commercial burglary, theft of documents, skimming and ram raiding, the latter being mostly committed by border region crime groups. However, the criminal repertory of itinerant crime groups does not stop there: particularly the highly structured groups are engaged in drug trafficking, trafficking in human beings, prohibited use of weapons and even violence and manslaughter.

5.4 Reasons for travelling

Itinerant crime groups engage mainly in systematically committing property crimes, but also in other aspects of the criminal perspective. True, they are organized, and some are more than others, but engagement in property crimes does not make them completely different from other criminal gangs or organizations. Spapens and Fijnaut (2005, p. 82) distinguish four offender types in their study on organized burglary. Next to itinerant crime groups – or mobile gangs – as they call them, professional thieves may also operate in groups and/or work in organized structures. The same counts for car theft and smuggling of stolen vehicles, another example of property crimes executed by criminal groups

(Bruinsma & Bernasco, 2004, p. 86; Spapens & Fijnaut, 2005, p. 98). Then what is it that makes these itinerant crime groups this special? Although choice of words varies to describe these groups, mobility is a recurrent issue. The question hereby, however, is how to understand this mobility. Is it a part of their lifestyle, are they travellers? In that case, one should avoid to generalize, as these people have to deal with presumptions as being criminal already (James, 2007). Or are they just mobile in their criminal behaviour, travelling further when committing crimes but not travelling as a way of life at all? The latter would mean they conflict with reigning criminological theories such as distance decay theory (see for example Rattner & Portnov, 2007; Rengert et al., 1999; Van Koppen & De Keijser, 1997). Ponsaers (2004) opted for the first option, stating that criminal behaviour of these groups challenges distance decay theory mainly because these offenders have no fixed residences, making it hard to assess their offending patterns.

Two main reasons for travelling are encountered. Our case file analysis showed that most offenders stay in Belgium illegally and only for rather short periods. This seems to confirm the travelling lifestyle hypothesis. However, looking at the individual offender is too limited and group offending cannot be explained by making the sum of all perpetrators individually (Tillyer & Kennedy, 2008, p. 81). Furthermore, certain offenders stay in Belgium for longer periods, trying to build a better life. They try to find jobs and only after a certain period – and because of financial pressure – become involved in crime.

Furthermore, even in cases where individual offenders do travel, often a certain group anchor point exists. In various groups, some key persons are active, living in Western Europe for a long time and providing a place to stay for offenders that only come over for a rather short period. From a group point of view, itinerant lifestyles account for only a part of these groups and we notice that most groups have certain fixed anchor points or regions.

Journey-to-crime calculations of offender groups in general cause problems, because distance should be measured from two points and mostly, operations will be located nearby the anchor point of one of the offenders (Bernasco, 2006, p. 147). For our subject groups, this is mostly no problem, as the starting point for one offender is the same or very nearby as for the others. In rare cases where more than one starting point was encountered, police investigations managed to clearly distinguish the relevant starting point.

5.5 Criminal fence

Itinerant crime groups travel large distances when committing crimes and this cannot be attributed to lack of fixed residences. Anchor point analysis shows that most groups have one or more offenders living in Belgium and/or connections with locally embedded people. This does not necessarily mean that all operations occur on a local or national level. In order to further assess mobility patterns, the relationships and fencing networks have been studied. These are not always investigation priorities and may therefore remain unclear in some cases. Nevertheless, some relevant information could be obtained. Lu (2003), in a study on vehicle theft, found that mobility patterns after crimes may as well reflect distance decay and be rather similar to traditional journey-to-crime patterns. The criminal fence can be an important factor in crime, because the relationship between the criminal receiver and the thief is essential for both parties. Nevertheless, attention for the criminal fence is rather limited. Sutton (1998) distinguishes five types of fencing markets, ranging from commercial sales to hawking, i.e. directly selling to consumers in clubs, pubs,...

Studies showed criminal receivers not always being professional receivers/criminals (Kruize, 2007, pp. 53-56) and fencing often occurring through informal ways (Kleemans, 1996, p. 71). Concerning the itinerant crime groups, some professional receivers were pictured. One case involved a fence dealing with expensive jewellery. In some other cases the fence took place in one or more pawnshops and for metal thefts, stolen goods are often sold to scrap dealers. This does not mean that these receivers are always aware of the criminal nature of the goods. Yet, while some cases involve professional receivers, most fencing activities take place through informal networks. These can be situated on a local level or abroad. Local fencing takes place through locally embedded persons or within the informal networks of the group (for example gypsy communities). In general, these groups steal easily disposable goods like jewellery, money and small electronics. One case involves a group being active in thefts of working tools. Buyers were then sought through a number of phone calls. In other cases, goods and vehicles were sold on second hand markets.

Most groups find ways to sell their stolen goods. Nevertheless, alternatives exist. First, some groups steal goods they do not have to sell, because they need not be sold. This can be the case for money, but also for small amounts of jewellery and small electronics. Typical for some of these groups, however, is that they steal consumables: food, drinks, cigarettes,... This is often the case for small, loosely structured groups and traveller clans (both Eastern European as indigenous). A second alternative is international fencing. A majority of the groups in our sample let the people in their home country benefit from their criminal behaviour. This includes transporting stolen goods (mostly by car) and stolen vehicles (mostly driven, rarely by boat), but also sending money home, often through money transfer companies. One should not forget that, although most groups have anchor points in Western Europe, the group members change. Thus, their family and sometimes even the centre of their own life, may still be situated in their home country. In this way, crime can be seen as an investment for a better life, both for them – whether or not they stay here for a longer time – and for their family (see also Segaert, 2006, p. 30). Rarely, criminal earnings are invested in further criminal activity.

Fencing activities for itinerant crime groups vary from own use and local activities through international fencing and letting the family benefit from the earnings. This variation offers opportunities to find out to what extent groups and group members still have connections with their home country and their degree of embedment in local society.

5.6 Risk management

As not all itinerant crime groups have a similar structure or composition, and they are active in various domains of property crimes and beyond, it comes as no surprise that methods and strategies differ as well. Part of this difference is related to crime type: commercial burglaries require more sophisticated or quicker methods (due to alarms) than most home burglaries, cars can be stolen either on the street by force or by stealing the keys inside the house first, the latter case being called 'garage theft', ram raids require cars and some degree of violence,... However, other strategies may differ as well. Offenders, just as their possible victims, engage in some form of risk management, trying to maximize their chances of success.

One of these strategies is preparation and planning. This occurs mostly in the case of more advanced forms of crime and/or specific targets (De Cock, 2006a, p. 47; 2007). After the decision to commit burglaries has been taken, there is often little or no further preparation. Bennett and Wright (1984, pp. 45-46) called this typology 'the search'. In their sample, nearly half of the offenders belong to this type. Other authors observed this typology as well, also in Belgium (see Verwee, Ponsaers, & Enhus, 2007, pp. 104-406). Repeat victimization occurs regularly. Six groups hit the same targets during their operations. Another group does not really target the same premises, but always targets the same type of holiday cottages, with exactly the same arrangement.

For burglaries, repeat victimization is not an exclusive operation method of these groups. On the contrary, re-victimization is quite common (Nee & Meenaghan, 2006, p. 946). Itinerant crime groups follow no totally different preparation scheme than other burglars either. What is rather typical, however, is that they often operate in series. One possible explanation for this serial behaviour is that they do not fear police action (De Cock, 2007). They do fear imprisonment, however, particularly if it were in their home country (De Cock, 2006a). As a consequence, various risk reducing measures have been observed. One often encountered strategy is reconnaissance activity, noticed in 18 out of 27 case files. The extent of reconnaissance varies. Most of them were performed shortly – one or a couple of days – before the crimes. Concerning residential burglaries, reconnaissance was, if present, often limited to a rather short exploration of the area, sometimes even by other people than those burgling. For commercial burglaries, this was more systematic: more information was obtained and targets were picked more carefully. One group had inside information on their targets and another had a map with all companies of their target type in Belgium and France.

Using strategies such as repeat victimization, planning, reconnaissance and mapping, these offender groups become familiar with their target areas and become aware of the features of their region of operation. Brantingham and Brantingham (1981b) defined the awareness space as the area of which offenders have knowledge. The gaining of this knowledge is based on both criminal and innocent activities (Brantingham & Brantingham, 1981b, p. 35). 'Innocent' activities can include work, school, shopping and leisure. Despite some exceptions, no information on 'innocent creation of awareness space' is known for these groups. Repeat victimization may be an explanation for further criminal activity, but it does not explain the initial criminal behaviour within a certain region. Because crime trips into unknown territories are relatively rare (Palmer, Holmes, & Hollin, 2002, p. 12; Van der Kemp & Van Koppen, 2007, p. 353), further research on the awareness space of these criminals is needed.

Next to the creation of awareness space and increasing knowledge on the target area, other risk management measures are encountered as well. Most groups use what we may call 'silent' strategies to avoid arrests: they reduce traceability by using phone cells, regularly changing SIM-cards and cell phones, use codes in conversation, use false identities and ID papers, destroy evidence, only commit crimes when the residents are absent (this is not new - see also Bennett & Wright, 1984, p. 94; Kleemans, 1996, pp. 53-54), minimize telephone contacts during the crimes, flee or temporarily stop criminal activity when they scent danger, use the way of least resistance and mislead potential victims. Violence towards victims is often not used or only to a limited extent, while internal violence is slightly more common. However, not all of them apply only silent/discrete strategies to reduce risks. One group committed one burglary in advance, in order to find out how long it would take the police authorities to arrive. Other groups block the road for police cars, act blatant in their criminal operations and threaten with or use violence against victims and/or police when pursued.

5.7 Towards a typology of itinerant crime groups

Various features have been attributed to itinerant crime groups. A qualitative case file analysis revealed a lot of variation, in organizational level, but also in offender characteristics, crime type, mobility, the criminal fence and risk management. In general, two main group types can be distinguished. On the one hand, we find the gypsy type groups, on the other the crime gangs. For each type, two extremes have been noticed. Thus, four extremes are observed, each with their own particular features (see figure 5.1). Although we have divided the itinerant crime groups into two main group types, this does not mean that there can be no mixed groups at all, but most of them will incline towards one or the other.

The first main type can best be describes as criminal communities. They have a clan wise structure and are characterized by a number of kinship relations: one or several families live together and know of each other's activities. They often form a part of the gypsy community, but it is important not to put them all in the same box: observed criminal activities should not lead to stigmatization of the whole gypsy community. Two subtypes have been noticed, each with their own specialization.

At the one extreme of the criminal communities we found the border region crime groups: small clans staying mostly in trailer camps in the border regions. These groups stay mostly within the same region. They are active in various types of property crimes, particularly including vehicle thefts and ram raids at both sides of the border. Their targets have often been repeatedly victimized and they make few efforts to stay unnoticed. When confronted with police, they flee, create distractions and try to eliminate their traces, for example by leaving/burning their cars and blocking the road for police vehicles.

At the other extreme, we found flexible gypsy groups. Some members stay within the same region, be it in trailer camps or in houses. These groups have international connections with other clans. This is observed in group membership (members being connected to several groups in various countries) and fencing activities (international fencing, making it difficult to trace the nature of certain goods). Flexibility is also observed in criminal behaviour: some of the groups are multi-criminal in a way that they do not only commit property crimes. Yet, there is more flexibility than this: whereas in other group types, crimes are almost exclusively committed by adult men, this is not the case here. Children and women are also sent out for stealing. Typical is that they avoid conflict, both with victims and with other actors such as witnesses or police. In order to do so, they use tricks and deception to gain access to houses and to rob people. Although cases are known of internal violence and conflicts, this is mostly not translated into violence towards victims, another example of their conflict-evading behaviour.

The second main type consists of crime gangs, not crime clans. Although some relatives may be encountered within a group, this is rather exceptional. These group members organize themselves not as a part of their lifestyle, but as part of their criminal behaviour. The reason for these groups to exist lies within their criminal actions. Again, two subtypes are observed, but here there is more of a continuum. The gypsy groups were both characterized by their own way of specialization. Within the crime gangs however, one type is clearly characterized by higher levels of organization, professionalism and specialization than the other.

At the low extreme we find groups of fortune-hunters. They have come over to Western Europe to create a better life back home. Some of them even did not know where to stay when they started their trip, some of them had a connection with someone here who was to provide temporary residences. They are loosely structured and, although they may have a criminal record back home, they are not specialized in particular crime types. Typical for this group type is the involvement in burglaries and car thefts, crimes for which only limited skills are required. From the group perspective, we often observe fixed anchor points in Belgium. From the perspective of the individual offender, however, temporariness is the key concept. Offenders of this fortune-hunter group type come over for short periods, regularly together with people they know, and return to their home country afterwards. They do not try to build up a life in Western Europe. This is reflected in the criminal earnings, which are transported to their home country. Relations with their homeland are vital and in several case files, offenders called their relatives using the phone in the house they burgled. Thus, there is an international perspective linked to these groups, but it is mostly bilateral:

only the country of origin and the country they operate are involved. This, amongst other things, distinguishes them from the second type of crime gangs.

Figure 5.1: Typology of ICG

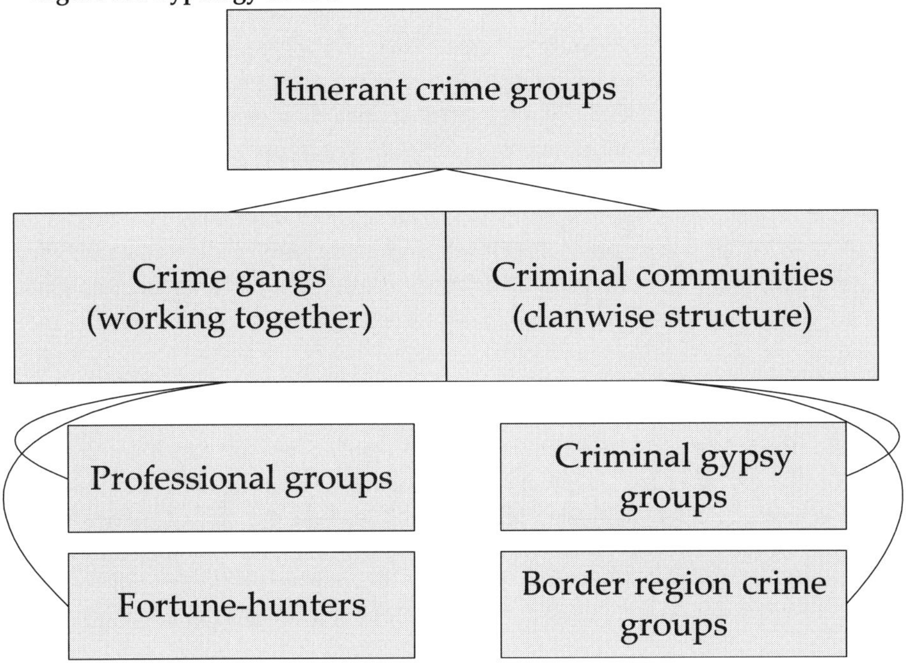

At the high end, we encounter highly professional and skilled groups. They engage in all sorts of criminal behaviour. Next to property crimes, links have been found with drug smuggling, trafficking in human beings, violence,... The heart of the structure lies not in the country of origin but in Western Europe. These groups have international connections as well. However, the connections here are multilateral and also linked to other Western European countries. Group members are changing, not because they return back home but because they are transferred to other groups. The Western European focus of these groups is also translated in the criminal fence. Goods are more likely to be sold in the West or transported via detours to the East, there is more investment in other criminal activities and items such as real estate, art and luxury goods. The reason they are brought under the heading 'itinerant crime groups' is mainly because of their Eastern European origin, not because of their itinerant/flexible behaviour.

5.8 Back to the definition

The Belgian definition of itinerant crime groups mentions a number of relevant issues to distinguish these groups. They are groups, originating mainly from the Eastern Bloc and committing a variation of property crimes. Other important aspects are their mobility, the fact that they operate from abroad or from the large Belgian conurbations, and the possible use of minors. As the police forces indicate themselves (De Raedt, 2006a, p. 23), this definition is based on empirical observations starting from the 1990s. Our case file analysis reveals that a high degree of variation is captured under the notion of 'itinerant crime groups'. Four main group types of itinerant crime groups have been observed. Linking the definition to the group types we encountered in our case file analysis, a number of questions are raised.

First, although border region crime groups are considered itinerant crime groups, one can ask whether this is truly the case. They are groups and are involved in property crimes. However, their operations are mainly limited to the border regions and as such, they are less mobile than the other types. They are also often Dutch or French instead of Eastern European. As mobility and nationality appear to be two important issues in the definition, one could wonder whether these border region crime clans are indeed itinerant crime groups.

Second, the definition mentions the possible use of minors. However, this has only been encountered in one type of groups. Although this aspect can be interesting to study, it is not a generally encountered feature of these groups. Therefore, including it in the definition may be confusing rather than clarifying.

Third, most groups – and certainly the large ones – are charged with being criminal organisations, and one could wonder whether there is an added value in another definition. Moreover, the emphasis in other countries is not always the same. In Germany (see for example Dortans, 2007), mobility is not really considered a determining issue, while in the Netherlands, the use of hit-and-run techniques is mentioned (Van der Laan & Weenink, 2005, p. 13), indicating short-term mobility and a very short stay in the target country – days instead of months. Thus, the phenomenon is addressed differently in the countries where it is observed, making comparisons and law enforcement cooperation more difficult.

Itinerant crime groups have increasingly gained attention by police forces in Western Europe, in this case Belgium. Policy makers have tried to put the phenomenon of Eastern European criminal gangs committing property crimes in a definition, but the scope of this definition is rather broad and not exhaustive, so it appears. A case file analysis of 27 groups shows large degrees of variation. There is heterogeneity in levels of organization, but also in offender characteristics, crime types, fencing, risk management and not to the least extent mobility. Because of these variations a further division into subtypes seemed appropriate. Criminal communities cannot be easily compared with Eastern European crime gangs and even within each type, the case files reveal large degrees of heterogeneity. There is one term used to describe these offender groups: 'itinerant crime groups'. However, our case file analysis shows that 'groups' are herewith interpreted in various ways, ranging from flexible, loosely structured to highly professional, 'crime' can be more than just property crimes and 'itinerant' is by no means straightforward, as many groups have fixed bases or even residences in Western Europe.

Chapter 6. Offender-based application of distance decay patterns[4]

Several studies on crime and place have identified a 'distance decay pattern' in which most crimes are committed near the offender's home, and the number of crimes declines as distances increase (see for example Phillips, 1980; Turner, 1969; White, 1932). This concept has two subdivisions, although these are rarely mentioned explicitly. First, most crimes are committed near home (i.e. offenders tend not to travel very far). Second, the distance curve shows decay, with the result that the number of crimes committed gradually reduces as distances increase.

Although distance decay is usually considered in relation to short distances, decline may also occur over long distances – decay refers to a distribution and is independent of absolute distance calculations. The primary concern of this chapter is therefore whether the number of offences reduces over longer distances on both the aggregate and the individual offender level. As such, this chapter contributes to a discussion about the application of the distance decay pattern (Rengert et al., 1999; Smith et al., 2009; Van Koppen & De Keijser, 1997) and to a better understanding of the distance decay pattern. It does so by splitting distance decay in its two components:

1. near-home offending: do offenders primarily operate within the vicinity of their homes, as many studies have found? (for a literature review, see Canter & Youngs, 2008a, pp. 4-6)
2. gradual decline: is there an even or an uneven distribution? Does the proportion of crimes wane with distance? (Canter & Youngs, 2008a, pp. 7-8)

Using mobility features from criminological literature, we compare mobility in terms of average distance travelled, with the mobility shown by specific types

[4] This chapter is an extended version of the paper:
Van Daele, S. (2010). Mobility and distance decay at the aggregated and individual level. In M. Cools, B. De Ruyver, M. Easton, L. Pauwels, P. Ponsaers, G. Vande Walle, T. Vander Beken, F. Vander Laenen, G. Vermeulen & G. Vynckier (Eds.), Safety, societal problems and citizens' perceptions: new empirical data, theories and analyses (pp. 41-59). Antwerp: Maklu.

of offender at the aggregate level. We expect more emphasis to be put on crimes further from home for these offenders, compared with the general pattern.

However, the average distance travelled to commit a crime is only a central measure and does not reveal any information on the actual shape of the distance decay curve. To flesh out the picture, therefore, we first explore whether high mobility actually results in different mobility patterns. In other words, does the distance decay curve of offences/offenders that are related to high mobility also show a deviating distance decay pattern, or is there straightforward decay, with the curve only slightly 'stretched' over the longer distance?

Second, we bring distance decay down to the level of the individual offender. Distance decay curves are often explored at the aggregated level (which often includes both near-home offending and decay), or central measures are used to calculate offender travelling behaviour, resulting in a loss of some interesting information (Brantingham & Brantingham, 1984b, pp. 222, 227). This is often done because listing a number of individual decay curves hampers a clear overall view of the data. In this chapter, instead of focusing on central measures, we measure decay itself – i.e. the distribution of distances travelled, independent of the offenders' mean distances travelled.

6.1 Distance decay

The principle behind the distance decay pattern is that criminals tend to commit most of their crimes close to home, and commit fewer crimes as distance increases. The greater the distance, the fewer the crimes committed. A distance decay curve can be created by counting and combining the individual distances between offenders' residence and the places where they carried out their crimes (Turner, 1969; Phillips, 1980). This curve is of a fairly standard shape. Nevertheless, the average distances vary in relation to the nature of the crime.

White (1932) observed in his sample an average distance of 2.7km for all types of criminality. He made the observation that crimes against people are committed very close to home (1.3km), while crimes against properties occur further away (2.8km). Other researchers have drawn similar conclusions. Phillips (1980, p. 175) found a mean average distance of 2.3km, ranging from 1.1km for assault to 1.7km for burglary, and 4km for petty larceny. Reppetto (1974) observed an average distance for burglary of only 0.8km. Capone and Nichols (1976, p. 209) concluded that average distances differ not only by type of crime, which in their study was robbery, but also in relation to type of target premises. The distances travelled to rob loan companies, for example, averaged 13.4km, while the average distance travelled to rob parking lots was only 3.5km. More recently, Wiles and Costello (2000) found a mean average distance of 3.1km, and in their study on serial arsonists Edwards and Grace (2006, pp. 223-224) found the mean distance travelled from the home base to the crime site was 6.6km. The distance decay curve actually has its origins in other sciences, such as biology, medicine and geography (see for example Mizutani & Jewell, 1998; Snow, 2008; Tobler, 1970), rather than in criminology.

The limited mobility of most offenders can be explained from a variety of perspectives. First, the rational choice perspective would indicate that costs and gains will be weighed against each other (Cornish & Clarke, 1986b). The actions that require least effort and result in maximum gains will be taken (see also Zipf, 1949). Travelling further takes more time, effort and cost (Pettiway, 1982, p. 257); for example, travelling longer distances means vehicles need to be used for longer periods of time, increasing the chances of arrest by routine police controls. There are few reasons to choose to travel longer distances if the benefits do not increase accordingly. This could explain why criminal mobility correlates with higher criminal achievements (Morselli & Royer, 2008; Snook, 2004, p. 62).

Second, everyday life influences offender mobility. Criminals will commit their crimes in areas where they also carry out other, non-criminal, activities. Brantingham and Brantingham (1981b) highlighted this pattern, and called it 'awareness space'. This is the total space an offender knows. Offenders are likely to perceive criminal opportunities when they are travelling about for other reasons. Most criminals will rarely decide to commit crimes in an area they have never been before, as without any form of reconnaissance they do not know the precise location of opportunities for crime, and have no knowledge of particular risks. Work and recreation are typical examples of non-criminal activities that help criminals to shape their awareness space and identify possible crime sites. Rengert and Wasilchick (1985, pp. 68-71) described these in their study on burglary. Offenders do not tend to commit their crimes when they are actually travelling for non-criminal purposes; instead, they notice opportunities when travelling, and feel safer when they are familiar with an area – which includes getting to know possible escape routes and dead-ends, and developing their risk perception. The authors narrow the concept of 'awareness space' further using the term 'search space', as not every part of the awareness space contains criminal opportunities (Rengert & Wasilchick, 1985, p. 55). Criminals first identify a suitable area that may provide an opportunity for crime, and then narrow their exploration down to potential targets (see also Bernasco & Nieuwbeerta, 2005). The more the space is narrowed, the more concrete criminal planning and operations become. After the principle of least effort, which is part of the rational choice perspective, Goodwill and Alison (2006, p. 408) consider anchoring and familiarity – what we call the influences of everyday life – as the most important issues in explaining criminal mobility.

A third influence is the existence of barriers. Elffers (2004) suggests that physical barriers, such as rivers, seas or forests limit travel options. Other authors have found that social (De Poot et al., 2005; Reynald et al., 2008) and even ethnic (Bernasco & Block, 2009; Gabor & Gottheil, 1984) barriers restrict offender mobility too.

The concept of limited offender mobility, and thus distance decay, is particularly useful in two fields. First, police authorities use it for geographical profiling, where a criminal's anchor point region is deduced from the location of several crimes (Besson, 2004, p. 145; Rossmo, 1995, 2000; Rossmo, Thurman, Jamieson, & Egan, 2008; Van der Kemp & Van Koppen, 2007). Specific computer software has been developed for this purpose, although the actual value of this software and its various functions has been the subject of considerable debate (Alison et al., 2003; Canter & Hammond, 2006, 2007; Paulsen, 2006; Snook et al., 2002; Snook et al., 2004; Snook, Zito, et al., 2005; Van der Kemp & Van Koppen, 2007). Moreover, some offenders act as criminal 'commuters' (Canter & Larkin, 1993). They operate around another anchor point than their residence, making it difficult to create a geographical profile.

Distance decay theory also proves useful in the field of theoretical criminological research. Different offence, offender and target types may influence the distance decay pattern (Bernasco, 2006; Bernasco & Block, 2009; Kocsis et al., 2002; Kocsis & Harvey, 1997; Pettiway, 1982; Santtila, Laukkanen, Zappala, & Bosco, 2008). However, the principle behind the distance decay pattern has also been the subject of debate. One discussion relates to the method used. As most papers in this field have been based on official police statistics, it may well be possible that people who commit crimes near home are more likely to be arrested, and thus the role of distance decay would be overestimated (Eck & Weisburd, 1995, p. 16; Laukkanen et al., 2008, p. 233). In other words, criminals who are more mobile may also be more successful and evasive, and are therefore less likely to be arrested (McIver, 1981, p. 43). In addition, not all criminals start their crime trip from home (Wiles & Costello, 2000, p. 40); however, most researchers assume they do, and therefore crime trip calculations may be biased.

A second issue relates to a discrepancy between the individual and the aggregate level. Van Koppen and De Keijser (1997) argued that the assumption of an individual distance decay function is an ecological fallacy. They modelled a number of offenders showing no individual distance decay pattern, resulting in a distance decay pattern on the aggregate level. They were criticised by Rengert, Piquero and Jones (1999) for their interpretation of the ecological fallacy, for neglecting the role of surface calculations over distances, for the interpretation of geographic work on profiling and for the assumption of random target selection. Nevertheless, this did not end the discussion over the role of the distance decay function. By using qualitative offender interviews, Polisenska (2008) put the near-home hypothesis in question, as she found that a number of burglars would travel considerable distances to commit their crimes. Smith, Bond and Townsley (2009, p. 217) also found that the aggregate distance decay function neglects the variation that exists between individual offenders' crime trip distributions.

In the present chapter, this second issue is tackled. The aim is to further improve the interpretation of the distance decay pattern. Two main hypotheses are formulated:

1. General distance decay neglects the differing patterns over distinguished groups. As such, larger average mobility may result in different decay patterns as well. Testing this hypothesis, we calculated such patterns for certain sections of offenders. Group divisions were based on a number of basic features and follow a suggestion made by Rengert et al., namely that "*[...] the next step is to identify how distance-decay parameters vary between groups of offenders (i.e., ethnicity, gender, region) and what that says about their offending behavior.*" (1999, p. 442)
2. Distance decay is mostly observed at the aggregate level. Assuming the presence of a similar pattern on the level of the individual offender is incorrect. In order to test this hypothesis, we measured individual decay using a method proposed by Smith et al. (2009, pp. 230-232).

6.2 Sample selection and skewness

With respect to the police data mentioned in the first chapters of the study, we use a two-sided approach. First, a number of aggregated distance decay curves were drawn. In this we were following Rengert et al.'s (1999, p. 442) suggestion that it is important to identify how distance-decay parameters vary between certain groups of offenders. The divisions are related to characteristics that literature suggests influence travel patterns and mostly in line with the ones described above:

- Multiple offending. Experienced offenders are found to travel further than other offenders (Barker, 2000; Beauregard et al., 2005, p. 587; Gabor & Gottheil, 1984). As our data set contains no information on prior convictions or arrests, we consider those offenders most experienced when they have committed 10 or more crimes in the period under consideration. This notion has been used before (Elffers, 2003; Ferwerda et al., 2003; Ferwerda et al., 1995; Smith et al., 2009, p. 224; Snook, Zito, et al., 2005). Although this approach is suitable when taking a general perspective, the possible impact of the law of small numbers forced us to only use these offenders in the second stage of analysis. Thus, this criterion merely provides information on the possible bias it generates when calculating individual decay patterns.
- Co-offending. Co-offenders are found to be more mobile than other offenders. They are likely to commit their offences near the residence of one offender, causing the other(s) who live elsewhere to travel longer distances (Bernasco, 2006, p. 147). Co-offending may increase the offenders' awareness space and enable them to travel further (Brantingham & Brantingham, 1981b; Gabor & Gottheil, 1984; Tremblay, 2004, p. 22).
- Eastern European offenders. Previous research has shown that Eastern European offenders tend to be more mobile compared with other offenders, particularly when they commit offences in Western Europe (Ponsaers, 2004; Van Daele, 2008; Van Daele, Vander Beken, & De Ruyver, 2008), although in Eastern European countries offenders generally appear to travel further to commit crimes (Polisenska, 2008).

For the present analysis, we also consider two additional variables: age and target affluence.

- Older offenders. Young offenders tend to commit more impulsive, opportunistic offences, and therefore travel shorter distances (Deakin, Smithson, Spencer, & Medina-Ariza, 2007, p. 54; Gabor & Gottheil, 1984, p. 270). Their choices are also affected by their reduced transport options (for example not having a driving licence). In this chapter we consider offenders older when they were aged 30 or over at the time of offence.
- Attractive targets. Mobile offenders often travel to attractive targets and richer neighbourhoods (Deakin et al., 2007, p. 65). Normally, targets in deprived areas are more at risk than those in affluent areas (Johnson & Bowers, 2004, p. 238). However, mobile criminals are more likely to travel to attractive targets further afield (Bernasco & Block, 2009, p. 98; Johnson & Bowers, 2004, p. 243; Maguire & Bennett, 1982, pp. 19-20). Mawby described this as 'rich pickings' (2001, p. 72). These offenders typically use arterial roads and major highways to reach affluent areas (Brantingham & Brantingham, 1984b, p. 357; Fink, 1969; Hakim, Rengert, & Shachmurove,

2000, p. 12; Kleemans, 1996, p. 192; Laukkanen et al., 2008, p. 232; Maguire & Bennett, 1982, pp. 41-42; Rossmo, 2000, p. 214). In order to measure the attractiveness of target areas, we used an affluence index designed by the Belgian National Institute for Statistics, in which every area with a wealth index above a mean of 100 is considered to be attractive.

We analyse whether our data confirms that offenders with these features showed increased mobility. We also consider whether this results in different travel patterns. To do this we analyse the aggregated distance decay curves of criminal actions containing these features, to see whether they deviate from the distance decay curve.

After comparing these aggregated distance decay curves, we take things further. On the individual level, most studies use mean distances to describe offending patterns. However, the distance decay curve would be more useful for this type of analysis (Smith et al., 2009, p. 220). One problem is how to measure decay patterns. Decay is often represented as a curve, which provides a whole range of information but leaves no room for further calculation; we therefore use a quantification of decay. This approach follows a method proposed by Smith, Bond and Townsley (2009, pp. 230-232), and uses the skewness scores of each individual decay curve. Skewness measures asymmetry, which is exactly what we are looking for in this approach. If skewness has a positive value, the right tail of a distribution is longer than the left. As distance decay illustrates most offences being committed near home (i.e. on the left side of the distribution), we expect most cases to be located on the left, and thus we expect distance decay to correspond with significant high skewness scores. In order to judge the significance of the individual decay curves, we work with the Z-scores of this skewness, which are calculated through dividing the skewness by its standard error. Only if this value differs more than 2 standard deviations from zero (greater than 1.96 or lower than –1.96) is the skewness significant.

Using one measure means that further calculations can be carried out and comparisons can be made. However, it is also likely to result in a loss of information, as patterns contain richer information than just single values (Brantingham & Brantingham, 1984b, p. 222; Rossmo, 2000, p. 101). Because this chapter attempts to compare the individual decay patterns of people from different groups that have been distinguished on the aggregate level, this loss of information may be regrettable but it does not hamper the outcome.

Skewness and their corresponding z score measure relative decay. They only consider the shape of the distance decay curve, not the distances that are observed within the curve. Thus, offender A who commits 8 offences at 2km and 2 at 10km from home will have a skewness z-score of 2.59, the same score as offender B who commits 8 offences at 4km and 2 offences at 20km from home.

The skewness score cannot be calculated for all offenders. In order to rule out small-number coincidences, only offenders who have committed 10 or more offences are taken into account. The first 5 offences are indicative for the range in which offenders operate (Barker, 2000, pp. 64-65), so it was imperative that this criterion is maintained. In order to outweigh overgeneralization, we only include offenders who have committed at least 10 offences from this stage on. This avoids a possible bias that could be generated by the law of small numbers. Given the similar curve that multiple offending generates in the first stage of the analysis, we do not expect to see differences by implementing this condition.

Second, skewness estimates cannot be calculated for those offenders who committed all their crimes in the same area. Those who commit crimes in the area where they live have been labelled 'marauders'; if it is another area they are 'commuters' (see Canter & Larkin, 1993). The nature of our dataset and the rough geographic variable allowed for no further specification within the boundaries of a particular municipality.

As with the first stage, we compare the individual decay results between our chosen groups with the general results for Belgium. This enables us to compare aggregated and individual decay, and addresses the question of whether mobility and decay are intertwined or relatively independent from each other.

6.3 Results

We first consider the mean distances travelled at the aggregate level, observing whether our chosen features result in higher mobility on the aggregate level. In general we notice a mean distance travelled of 19.1km. This is substantively higher than the results found in literature. However, as most other studies have been executed on city level, not country level, these studies exclude travelling across city borders. Calculating the median distance, we find an average of 7.2km, indicating that our first calculation is certainly influenced by a number of extreme values (we observed a number of crime trips over 250km, which is more or less the maximum distance that can be travelled in Belgium). We then calculate the mean and median distance travelled for each chosen feature. (see Table 6.1).

Table 6.1: Distances travelled and 'mobility features'

Mobility characteristics	N	Mean distance (km)	Median distance (km)
Multiple offenders	18,755	24.4	11.1
Co-offenders	41,590	20.1	7.2
Eastern European offenders	7,078	34.7	22.1
Offenders age 30+	16,496	22.1	8.9
Attractive targets	31,569	20.1	8.6
All	*67,981*	*19.1*	*7.2*

Although correlations between travelled distance and these features are negligible, absolute figures indicated a slightly higher mobility for all features except one. This first step shows that these features do result in higher offender mobility than the average for Belgium, though the difference is only slight for some features. A next step, however, is whether these higher central values of mobility (mean and median) are also accompanied by different distance decay curves.

In order to keep the curves comparable, we divide the distances travelled into bands of 10km. The first band contains all crimes committed at less than 10km from an offender's residence, the second includes the crimes committed from 10 to 19km, and so on. As very few offences are committed over 100km from an offender's residence, we only include distances of less than 100km. Because the used branches are not detailed, we overcome some of the interpretation problems that may be caused by working only with municipality coordinates. Moreover, because even such rough distinction shows a lot of variation and corresponding distance decay curves, the measure – despite its roughness – is adequate for the framework of this chapter.

Figure 6.1 illustrates that the pattern of most offender groups follows a distance decay pattern, regardless of their higher mobility. One pattern deviates from this – Eastern European offenders tended to be less likely to offend within the 10km range from home (32%, compared with percentages of at least 47%, but mostly over 50%, for the other groups). They also commit many more offences over 20km from their residence. Thus, the distance decay pattern for Eastern European offenders appears to be less straightforward than it is for other offenders.

This exercise shows that particular groups of offenders are indeed more mobile, as indicated by previous research, but that higher mobility rarely implies different decay curves. Apart from Eastern European offenders, most offence patterns show a quite steep level of decay, even with their higher level of mobility. Eastern European offenders show an existing but modest decay pattern, with fewer offences committed within 10km and more at distances over 20km from the residence.

Figure 6.1: Aggregated distance decay patterns

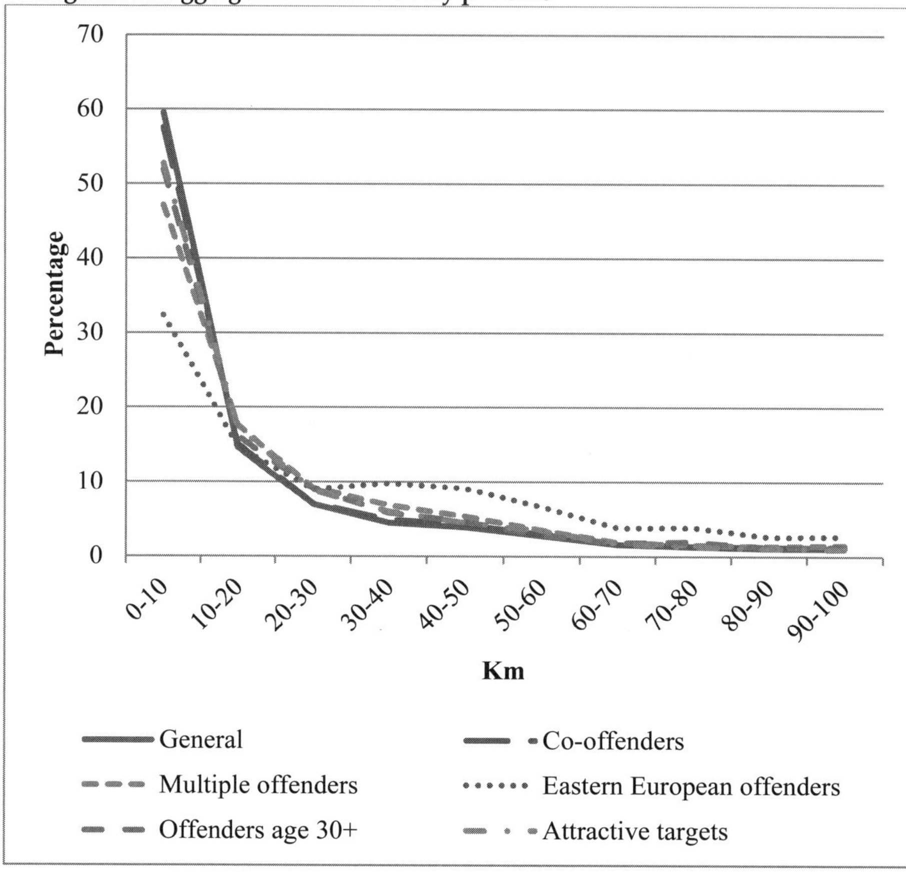

This approach uses offender–offence combinations as the unit of analysis. Although it has also been used by other authors (see for example Hodgson & Costello, 2006; Kleemans, 1996), we admit it is a slightly unusual approach. Most studies use either the offence or the offender as the unit of analysis. If the offender alone is analysed, features that are linked to the offence are excluded, and vice versa. Working with offender–offence combinations allows characteristics of both the offender and the offence to be included in the analysis.

Although the presence of a distance decay pattern is widely accepted within criminological research, it is often observed at the aggregate level and there is an ongoing discussion about whether it can also be observed at the offender level

(Rengert et al., 1999; Smith et al., 2009; Van Koppen & De Keijser, 1997). Taking into account the observed variations on the aggregated level, we compare these results with an individual measure of decay. It is important to bear in mind that this only measures decay and does not test the near-home hypothesis. Thus, offenders can be quite mobile, still following a decay pattern, or can commit most offences in a limited area but without any particular decay. We may calculate mean skewness, but this again eliminates individual variations.

Co-offending and the choice of attractive targets refer to offence characteristics and not offender features. We therefore define offenders as co-offenders when they commit more than half of their crimes with other offenders. When the mean attractiveness score of a target area is higher than the overall mean – higher than 100 – we consider offenders to be heading for attractive targets.

On the individual level, only a minority of offenders show straightforward distance decay, meaning they have a skewness z-score above 1.96. Depending on which offenders are considered, only 38.5–49.4% show distance decay in the strict sense. For about 25%, we find decay, but cannot determine whether this is significant. For another 14–20% we find a distance increase, but again cannot determine its significance. Nevertheless, we find that 10% of the offenders show a significant negative skewness, meaning that they follow a distance increase instead of a distance decay pattern.

Table 6.2: Individual decay

	Valid	Mean	Skewness Z (row percentages)			
			> 1.96	> 0 and < 1.96	< 0 and > –1.96	< –1.96
All multiple offenders	765	2.10	49.4	24.7	14.1	11.8
Co-offenders	485	2.04	48.5	26.6	15.5	9.5
Eastern European offenders	122	1.67	38.5	31.1	19.7	10.7
Offenders age 30+	155	1.84	45.8	25.8	18.1	10.3
Attractive targets	365	1.94	46.0	25.5	16.2	12.3

On the individual level, only a minority of offenders show straightforward distance decay, meaning they have a skewness z-score above 1.96. Depending on which offenders are considered, only 38.5–49.4% show distance decay in the strict sense. For about 25%, we find decay, but cannot determine whether this is significant. For another 14–20% we find a distance increase, but again cannot determine its significance. Nevertheless, we find that 10% of the offenders show a significant negative skewness, meaning that they follow a distance increase instead of a distance decay pattern.

For 15.2% of the offenders the skewness cannot be determined, because they committed all offences within the same area. For the respective subtypes of offenders, this ranges from 4.9% for Eastern European offenders to 14.5% for offenders heading for attractive targets. This also implies that Eastern European offenders and offenders aged 30 or older have a wider spread of target areas than co-offenders and offenders heading for attractive targets.

6.4 Aggregate vs. individual decay

At the aggregate level, we notice quite a large variation in mean distance travelled, ranging from 19.1km in general to 34.7km for Eastern European offenders. This results in differences in distance decay patterns. However, apart from Eastern European offenders, where distance decay deviate slightly more (fewer offences were committed at distances of less than 10km), decay variations appear to be more or less in line with the general distance decay pattern. Thus, at the group level, near-home offending and decay are intertwined to a large extent, as higher mobility leads to slightly less decay. In other words, longer distances travelled result in a distance decay pattern that is slightly stretched to the right. At least, this is what we observe at the aggregate level.

At the individual level, the pattern appears to be less straightforward. By using the skewness z-scores of offenders' decay curves, we calculate the individual level of decay. The result is a relative measure, only focusing on the distribution of decay itself: skewness is independent from mean distance travelled and, therefore, from near-home offending.

Although most offenders tend to commit their crimes near home, this does not always translate into a decay curve at the individual level. About half of the offenders show a pattern of distance decay at the individual level. Moreover, for every 5 offenders following a clear distance decay pattern, 1 follows a significant distance increase pattern. For Eastern European offenders and offenders systematically heading for attractive targets, this odds ratio becomes 4 to 1.

As z-scores significance is subject to the standard error, we wonder whether individual distance decay variations are partially due to the skewness standard error. The standard error for $z > 0$ is similar to that for $z < 0$ (respective means of

0.56 and 0.57; assumed equality $p<0.05$). For significant and insignificant z-scores (z falling outside or inside the –1.96 to 1.96 span), however, we observe significant differences (respective means of 0.55 and 0.58; $p<0.01$). This shows that z-score significance may indeed be biased by the standard error of the individual distributions.

As the standard error is strongly correlated with the number of crimes committed ($r=0.797$, $p<0.01$), we also control for additional bias by taking into account the number of crimes individual offenders committed. We find that offenders with significant distance decay commit more crimes on average than those who follow significant distance increase patterns (respective means of 23.5 and 21.0). Yet these differences are not significant ($p=0.22$). Neither standard error differences nor differences in the average number of committed crimes can falsify our finding that for every 5 offenders showing a distance decay pattern, there is at least 1 who shows a distance increase pattern.

Within our subgroups, co-offenders tend to be most likely to follow distance decay. This is rather unexpected. After all, offending perpetrated in a group setting often cannot be explained by simply the sum of individual rationality (Tillyer & Kennedy, 2008, p. 81). Co-offenders are likely to commit their crimes near the residence of one offender (Bernasco, 2006, p. 147). This would mean that for crimes that are committed near the residence of offender A, we would not expect straightforward decay for offender B. If all co-offended crimes were committed by two offenders, this would mean that at least half of the offenders are likely to show no decay pattern, and as some crimes are committed by more than two offenders, this percentage should be even higher. Before any hasty conclusions are drawn, however, the reader should consider the following three points.

First, skewness estimates cannot be calculated for 14.4% of the co-offenders. Together with those offenders heading for attractive targets, this is substantially higher than it is for Eastern European offenders (4.9%) and offenders aged over 30 (6.5%). Thus, co-offenders who commit all offences in the same area, which may well be the resident area of one of the co-offenders, are excluded from the analysis.

Second, co-offenders may live near each other, making their decay patterns resemble each other, particularly at our level of analysis. For 53% of the crimes that are committed by two or more offenders, at least two offenders lived in the same area. Thus, for over half of the co-offended crimes, the anchor point of one offender was the same as for at least one other offender. In these cases, the fact that co-offenders tend to commit their crimes near the anchor point of one participant does not influence the individual decay pattern.

Third, co-offending networks are by no means fixed and not all co-offenders are multiple offenders. In fact, only 23.6% of co-offended crimes are committed by criminals who are classed as multiple offenders. Individual decay patterns are only calculated for multiple offenders. As these offenders are more experienced than others, they may have more discretionary power in the choice of target area, and therefore may choose to offend near their own residence. This behavioural model could apply for 76.4% of the co-offended crimes.

Taking into account these three points, we believe the relatively large proportion of individual decay among co-offenders is not contradictory to previous findings. Because of their relativity, skewness z-scores by no means contradict the fact that the majority of crimes are committed near home. On the contrary, their main value lies in cutting decay loose from near-home offending. Also, like mean distance, this is only one value. It reveals some of the information that is lost when discussing mean distance, but does not provide as much information as a distance decay curve. Unfortunately, this appears to be the price to be paid for working with comparable and quantifiable values. In addition, it only takes into account information on the crimes, and neglects the environmental backcloth (see Brantingham & Brantingham, 1993a). Intervening opportunities (Elffers, Reynald, Averdijk, Bernasco, & Block, 2008; Stouffer, 1960), awareness space (Brantingham & Brantingham, 1981b), search space (Rengert & Wasilchick, 1985) and incorrect anchor point perception (Wiles & Costello, 2000) are not considered. Yet this is also the case for most journey-to-crime research using mean distance travelled.

In this chapter we use Belgian municipalities as a unit of analysis. This related to the nationwide data used, the emphasis on mobile offenders within the broader framework this chapter is situated in, and the importance of municipalities from theoretical, methodological and policy perspectives (Hardyns & Pauwels, 2009, pp. 169-171). However, this also implies a loss of information at smaller levels of offender mobility. For a number of offenders, skewness estimates and skewness z-scores cannot be computed, because they have committed all offences in the same area. 73.3% of them committed the offences in their home area. A further division of geographic locations may clarify the decay patterns of these offenders as well. Future research could therefore work with exact address locations in order to calculate distances more precisely. This could rule out any possible bias due to the level of analysis.

This chapter considers variations in individual decay patterns. It is important, particularly from a theoretical perspective, that we have established that these differences do exist. By providing evidence that supports the conclusion of Smith et al. (2009) that individual differences in distance decay are often lost if analysed only at the aggregate level, we hope to contribute to the discussion about whether distance decay can be applied at the level of the individual offender.

Future steps could contribute to the journey-to-crime research from both a theoretical and a policy perspective. From a theoretical perspective, it is important to explore whether an increase in the distance travelled to commit a crime is accompanied by a directional bias. This would enable the principles of geographic profiling to be either questioned or supported. If decay variations are combined with directional bias, establishing a geographical profile would become difficult for this type of offender. If, however, distance increase curves show limited directional bias, this would mean that even for these offenders, offence locations are mainly spread around the anchor point. In that case, such offenders could be geographically profiled in the traditional way.

From a policy perspective, added value could be found in investigating why offenders decide to travel further, even if they know of and have experience of targets nearby. Is this the result of successful preventive measures close to the residence, forcing offenders to travel more, or is it merely influenced by locations further afield being more attractive or less risky? A next step could therefore be to explore whether decay is a function of target features, offender characteristics and the environmental backcloth.

This chapter explores two main issues. We are interested in mobile offending and want to establish whether high mobility is accompanied by different mobility patterns. We therefore select some features of mobile offending from literature and find that these do result in higher average distances travelled in our sample. Yet, higher mobility does not necessarily lead to different distance decay distributions: slightly fewer offences appear to be committed within 10km of home, but nevertheless a clear distance decay pattern is observed. Only in the case of Eastern European offenders does this turn out not to be the case: the percentage of offences committed by Eastern European offenders near to their homes is found to be considerably lower than for other offenders, and they commit more crimes at distances of 20–40km from their residence than did other offenders. Although some decay is still observed, it is less straightforward for this subgroup.

Establishing distance decay patterns reveals two main issues. On the one hand, it turns out that higher mobility does not always lead to notably different distance decay patterns. Thus, high mobility does not necessarily equal different mobility. On the other hand, even some basic group divisions, such as nationality, can result in deviating distance decay patterns. Even at the aggregate level, taking the universality of the distance decay pattern for granted is questionable, which is confirmed by the skewness z-scores for the 'Eastern European' and the 'aged above 30' subgroups. Variations do indeed exist, and can reveal interesting information if group divisions are well chosen in respect of the crime being studied.

Additionally, we attempt to translate aggregated distance decay patterns into individual distance decay patterns, by calculating individual skewness z-scores. The results were given for each offender type and revealed that fewer than half of the offenders followed a significant distance decay pattern. At the other end of the spectrum we found a distance increase pattern among over 10% of offenders.

Although distance decay can clearly be seen at the aggregated level, at the level of the individual offender it is less apparent. Eastern European offenders differ most from the general pattern in the first analysis. At the offender level, they are less likely to show significant decay, but tend to compensate this with non-significant decay patterns.

The results appear to confirm those of Smith et al. (2009), namely that substantial variation is hidden when only aggregated distance decay patterns are considered. At the aggregated level, the pattern of decay turns out to be a consequence of near-home offending. At the offender level, this is no longer the case. Skewness z-scores indicate that decay is not the simple result of offender mobility. Skewness may therefore function as a measure to estimate the travel patterns of an individual offender. It is important to clarify whether one is measuring distances travelled (i.e. investigating near-home offending), or decay patterns, and to keep them both separated, as the connection they show on the aggregated level cannot easily be seen on the level of the individual offender.

Chapter 7. The anchor points of itinerant crime groups[5]

As we have demonstrated above, being 'mobile' is, within criminal perspective, rather strange and deserves further attention. Its easiest conception, mobility – as with travelling and distance – requires a starting point, a certain journey, and an end point. Most studies focus on the journey itself. However, it is important to make sure the actual starting point is perceived correctly. While home is (too?) often considered the logical anchor point of crime travelling behaviour, this could eventually prove to be incorrect. The central question of this chapter is therefore whether high offender mobility is derives from flexibility in this starting point. This is necessary in order to see whether apparently mobile offenders are indeed that mobile, and to find out whether a wrong interpretation of the starting point can to some extent explain certain degrees of observed mobility.

7.1 Relevance of anchor points

In a criminal context, mobility can be regarded in terms of triangles (Rand, 1986; Tita & Griffiths, 2005, p. 277). Hereby, a triangle formed by offender residence, victim residence and place of offence is considered. These triangles can differ significantly. For certain crimes, for example stranger rape, all three features will be located in a different census tract, while for domestic violence all three will be located in the same census tract. For property offences, targeted in this chapter, offender residence and place of offence will be different, with victim residence located in the same census tract of the place of offence (for example burglary) or in a third census tract. As this chapter focuses on offender mobility, it is the distance between offender and offence location that matters.

---

[5] A preliminary version of this chapter has been published as:
Van Daele, S. (2009). Itinerant crime groups: mobility attributed to anchor points? In M. Cools, S. De Kimpe, B. De Ruyver, M. Easton, L. Pauwels, P. Ponsaers, G. Vande Walle, T. Vander Beken, F. Vander Laenen & G. Vermeulen (Eds.), Contemporary issues in the empirical study of crime (Vol. 1, pp. 211-225). Antwerp: Maklu.

Research on criminal mobility mostly examines the distance between offender residence and offence. This is, according to Ponsaers (2004, p. 19), one of the problems in targeting itinerant crime groups. Their travelling behaviour seems to conflict with criminological theories on criminal mobility, because they have no real residence. This can be confirmed in two ways. First, police studies both in Belgium and the Netherlands have showed that these Eastern European multiple offenders mostly come to Western Europe for very short periods, using hit-and-run techniques (Van der Laan & Weenink, 2005, p. 13) and/or staying here illegally (Dienst voor het Strafrechtelijk Beleid, 2005, pp. 30-34). Second, this has also been recorded empirically. In general, for only 48.2% of the offenders was their real residence known. We expect that this will be higher for Belgian offenders than it will be for foreigners. Foreigners are more likely to stay in Belgium illegally, making it harder for authorities to register where they live. Because they often live together with or near other companions, they will not be likely to provide information on their residence. This expectation is confirmed by our data: 52.6% of the Belgian offenders have a known real residence. For foreigners, this figure is only 39.3%. However, what we did not expect was a difference within the group of foreigners: only 35.8% of the Eastern European offenders have known real residences, while this figure rises to 41.2% for other foreign offenders. Thus, Eastern European offenders are less likely to have a straightforward residence in Belgium than other offenders – both Belgian and foreign – have.

Based on both police studies and our data, it is fair to say that assessing the distance between residence and offence location is less obvious for Eastern European multiple offenders than it is for other offenders. However, considering residence as starting point for criminal behaviour is not always correct. Wiles and Costello (2000, p. 48) found that criminals do not always start from home. They might also start from elsewhere, particularly leisure locations but also friends' residences. Instead of using residence as starting point, Rengert (1992, p. 110; 2004, pp. 169-170) considers what he calls 'anchor points'. This, together with travel direction and distance, determines the journey to commit crime (Rengert, 2004). In a majority of cases, this anchor point will still be the home residence of the offender. Yet, room is left open for other interpretations.

Taking into account the possibility that other places than residence may function as anchor points and given the fact that the often used distance between residence and offence location provides only limited and atypical results for Eastern European multiple offenders, it may be worthwhile to look more deeply into the interpretation of the anchor points of these offenders. The anchor point and interpreting it correctly has important implications for crime travelling and, thus, offender mobility conclusions, including distance decay.

7.2 Assessment

It would lead us too far to summarise the concept of 'anchor points' of all 27 case files studied. Instead, we have selected four cases which deserve special attention for mobility reasons. Four main types of anchor points have been found throughout the files and are reflected in these four cases. We have named each of them accordingly. From each case file, we extract the Eastern European multiple offenders. We are unable to automatically link the perpetrators from the files with the offenders from our database, because we only obtained the offender codes in the database and not their real names. By looking at the crimes in the files and their respective dates, this link is established manually. We then compare whether these offenders have a registered residence in the database, whether these residences are the same and whether these residences function as anchor points for these criminals. Because this chapter is of a qualitative nature, no quantitative conclusions should be drawn.

7.2.1 Case 1: Group residence as starting point

The first case deals with a group involved in committing commercial burglaries. The group is of Georgian origin and committed property crimes in several supermarkets of the same store chain. They reside in a city in the centre of Belgium, from which they operate. One offender lives in Belgium and offers the others – who tend to often move between Belgium and Georgia – a place to stay. The group consists of five property offenders. The case file indicates four multiple offenders. In the database, however, only three of them are retrieved. Two of them are registered in the anchor point city, the residence of the third one is unknown. Considering the group as one entity, the average travelled distance for the group is 44km.

This group type comprises the majority of cases in our sample. Mostly there is one offender who is embedded in the local society and lives in Belgium. He offers the other offenders a place to stay. The offenders mostly live together, nearby or even with the embedded offender. One case was slightly different, in a way that the group managed to force themselves into the house of a man, who was not an offender and not part of the group. In another case, not one, but two houses next to each other were used. Although the group composition may fluctuate, the premises stay the same and are linked to one person– often an offender – living in Belgium.

7.2.2 Case 2: Different anchor point than residence

One of the larger cases deals with a group responsible for over 400 burglaries and attempted burglaries. The group consists of 7 multiple offenders. The majority are of Yugoslavian nationality, although a Georgian and a Czech perpetrator are part of the group as well. Three criminals have a registered residence in Antwerp, which is one of Belgium's major cities. Their mean travelled distances are 10km, 38km and 67km. From the case file, it appears that the group started their crime trips in a pub in Antwerp and returned there afterwards. Thus, Antwerp can be considered the anchor point for the group. If we calculate distances from this anchor point, the offenders without registered residence travel respectively 16km, 25km, 26km and 65km on average.

Although slightly similar to the above-mentioned case, there are some differences. Here, the number of offenders staying at the same premises is rather limited. A whole number of premises are known, each housing one or two offenders. These premises are linked to their residents, not to one offender with connections in the region. Offenders in this case have a longer history in the country and might be bound more to local structures. Therefore, they may be limited to some sort of awareness space (see Brantingham & Brantingham, 1981). For this type, there is no central residence to function as an obvious anchor point. In the above-mentioned case, a pub turned out to be the central point for offenders to meet, start their crime trips and bring in the loot.

7.2.3 Case 3: Semi-residential or semi-sedentary

Another encountered case refers to a Yugoslavian Roma group of nearly 30 offenders, showing various levels and kinship ties. Flexibility is observed in various ways. First, it is not a straightforward itinerant crime group, in that its composition is rather atypical. Not all of the perpetrators have an Eastern European nationality. Three Eastern European multiple co-offenders are observed. While most itinerant crime groups consist of slightly older (born in 1977 on average), male offenders, this is not the case here. Some offenders are considerably younger. Two minors have already been registered for 7 offences. It is also noteworthy that one of the three core itinerant offenders is female. Second, flexibility and variety is also observed in residence location. A number of residences are located in the region of Charleroi. However, if we look at the registered residences in our database, we notice that this city is only mentioned for one of the three multiple offenders. For one other perpetrator the residence is unknown and the third offender's residence was registered in Germany. This does not necessarily mean that this is wrong. Police investigations have found that crime trips started from Charleroi and most offenders live there as well. It is possible that others also stay there, be it only for a while. If we change all residence locations to the found anchor point, we notice mean distances of 107km for the offender registered in Charleroi, 103km for the female offender and 84km for the 'German' offender (155km if counted each time from the German border). Given the principles of distance decay, it is quite likely that the residence might indeed not be Germany or that this offender has at least stayed in both places for some time.

This case reveals that conclusions about exact residences are difficult to draw, certainly when dealing with flexible groups. However, most groups of this type move around, but also stay within a certain region or close to a certain city. Although they have an itinerant lifestyle, they may be somewhat embedded in local reality due to this semi-residential nature. They do commit crimes far away – as in the above-mentioned case – or even abroad. Both their lifestyle and criminal operations make it difficult for police authorities to target them. Yet, these problems should not lead to a perception of itinerant people as criminal by definition (James, 2007).

7.2.4 Case 4: multiple temporary operating bases

An example of this group type counts just above ten Romanian or Moldovan property offenders. Seven of them are multiple offenders. The group operates in a number of crime waves. During these waves, the group members intensively commit burglaries. Their main targets are houses, business and sport clubs. They operate nearly every night and sometimes even commit about ten crimes in one night. They also engage in (near) repeat burglaries. The waves each take about a month. All of a sudden a wave stops, just to start again one month later. Because there were manifold contacts with people in their home country, one can assume that they briefly return to Romania in between. Two perpetrators were observed in all three crime waves. They start together, but are afterwards accompanied by respectively one (first wave), two (second wave) and another two (third wave) multiple offenders. Other, non-multiple offenders, join the group now and then as well, albeit it in a less structured way. Probably because they return to their home country in between, their anchor points in Belgium are not really fixed. For one offender, the registered residence is located in Romania while for the others, it is unknown in the database. In the case file, more residences are known these being abroad. Yet, as they are active each single night during their crime waves, it is virtually impossible for them to return every night. As it is unclear how to establish the time span in which each anchor point is used, minimum distances are calculated for all offenders. Thus, the distance to the closest anchor point is used. This reveals a group mean distance travelled of 13km. On the offender level, the following mean distances are observed: 10km for the offender who is only active during the first wave, 15km for offenders mostly active during the second wave, 5km for offenders mainly active during the third wave and 13km for offenders being active during all three crime waves.

This group combines a middle term hit-and-run technique with utilisation of different anchor points and difficult-to-assess crime patterns. This type of group sometimes only stays in Belgium for certain periods. They tend to search for possible anchor points and, once found, travel across a large region in search of targets. If we assume that crimes have been committed from the nearest anchor point, this group does not travel larger distances than non-itinerant offenders. This does not mean that the closest anchor point is valuable for every crime. This approach therefore probably underestimates distances to some extent. However, if we were to use the mean distance from the offence location to the various anchor points, i.e. every anchor point having equal chances to be the starting point for this crime, the group's mean travelled distance would raise to 35km, which is comparable to what we have noticed as our database mean for itinerant crime groups. This case shows that detailed assessment of temporary residences can sometimes lead to other conclusions concerning travelling.

7.3 Back to offender mobility

In our case file analysis, we reveal four types of anchor points. Some groups do indeed use several anchor points. It can only be estimated where they have stayed in which period, based on time of discovery and the goods found in each base. This makes it very difficult to assess their crime travelling as such. The other groups do indeed use anchor points that can be assessed. Some of them are semi-residential, but mainly stay in the same vicinity, making it possible to target this region as an anchor point. Other groups consist of offenders temporarily living in Belgium. A part of them stays and lives in Belgium for a longer period. They each live in separate premises, using a nearby starting point for their crime trips. The majority of groups, however, include at least one offender living in Belgium who provides a place to stay to other group members. The composition of this last group type varies. Crime trips are herewith best analysed not on an offender level, but on group and anchor point level, as these anchor points tend to remain active during the period of activity.

The awareness space and actual crime travelling of itinerant crime groups can be linked to several features. Groups that have connections with locally embedded people may search for targets in the awareness space of these people. Groups with connections abroad and without fixed residences may have a different distance perception, which would explain their crime travelling. Groups with no bonding at all to local reality may form their awareness space during their criminal operations, which possibly explains their engagement in (near) repeat burglaries. Finally, awareness space cannot only be created in a real way, but may also be formed in an artificial way.

Using the known anchor points to calculate travelling activity still results in large crime trips for most groups. Yet, this does not mean that there is no awareness space (see Brantingham & Brantingham, 1981b) or search space (Rengert & Wasilchick, 1985). Groups of types 1, 2, and even 3 may be locally embedded to some extent. At least some of the people connected to the group actually live here. Thus, a local embedding, not necessarily of the perpetrators themselves, but at least of someone with close connections to the group, is established. It is therefore possible that the people with local knowledge are involved in target (area) choice. Here, it is of vital importance to distinguish the locations from where the crime trips start and not take the place of residence for granted as the anchor point. This does not solve the question as to why they travel larger distances: on the contrary. With the observation of local connections, we could expect local operations. Still, large degrees of mobility were observed in criminal activity.

Offenders of the third type tend not to be bound to local reality, although they do have connections with locals. These groups also have links with various countries abroad, possible perceiving distances in a broader and less restrictive way. For the other group types, we notice various means of awareness space expansion. Some groups use reconnaissance techniques. This is mostly applicable for travelling towards high profit targets (see Morselli & Royer, 2008). In our sample, this is mostly the case for commercial burglaries – where the loot is probably indeed higher - rather than domestic burglaries. Other groups are characterised by large degrees of (near) repeat victimisation (see for example Bowers & Johnson, 2005; Palmer et al., 2002, p. 9; Townsley, Homel, & Chaseling, 2003) whilst for one group, the police during their investigation even found a map containing the locations of all supermarkets of the target type in France and Belgium.

What are the implications of this case file analysis? Eastern European multiple offenders tend to travel further than other offenders. This observation still stands when the anchor points are subjected to a more profound analysis. Thus, paying special attention to these groups from a police perspective seems well-founded. However, the case file analysis reveals that the notion 'itinerant crime groups', which implies a travelling life style, may not be that well-chosen. Although the individual offenders often travel, the group bases as such mostly stay within the same city/region. Eastern European multiple offenders create particular challenges both for law enforcement agencies and criminologists. From a criminological point of view, the next step is to see whether other features may explain the larger distances travelled. From a law-enforcement perspective, attention can and should be paid to the anchor points. Due to the flexible nature of these groups, a purely offender-related approach may miss certain opportunities. When aiming at these anchor points, however, the group perspective provides opportunities to reduce the local connections. By taking out those persons locally embedded and providing places to stay, group operations can – at least temporarily – be hampered.

Crime distances are often assessed by mean travelled distances. This involves information on both starting point and offence location. For property crimes, the place of offence is mostly clear. This is not always the case for the starting or anchor point. This seems to be confirmed by the rather low number of residences of Eastern European multiple property offenders that have been registered in the police database.

We analyse some case files of these itinerant crime groups, in order to find out whether this problem is inherent to these groups. The question is raised as to whether they do indeed not have clear anchor points which we can assess. Either the residences are not registered because they cannot be pinpointed (for example through the use of temporary operating bases), or their registration in the database is hampered by other features (for example illegal residence). Because residence is not always the anchor point, traditional distance calculations should be assessed with care.

However, the vast majority of these groups do have assessable anchor points to some extent, at least on a group level. The anchor points are often fixed, mostly houses/apartments provided by people living in Belgium. Sometimes operations start from a pub or other place than residence, functioning as anchor points. For those who do not have fixed residences, there is always a region from which the group operates and this region does not change that much.

Thus, was Ponsaers (2004) right when he stated that the operations of itinerant crime groups seem to conflict with reigning criminological literature? This chapter shows he was, although to another extent than he expected. It is not impossible to assess these groups' journeys to commit crime – it requires more information than just crime statistics, though – but even when analyzed more thoroughly, the problems still stand: these groups do indeed travel far and this cannot be attributed to the conception of their anchor points.

Chapter 8. Outbound offenders and their operation methods[6]

The city has long played a central role in environmental criminology, from analysis of offender residences in cities to identifying crime hot spots and patterns of urban and suburban crime. However, other crime patterns, with links to the city, can also be observed. Some ethnographic analyses have noticed patterns of criminals heading for affluent target areas near to, but clearly outside, city boundaries. The aim of this chapter is to take this exploration one stage further by analysing these crime trips that start in a city – in this case Brussels – but end outside it. As such, this chapter leaves aside the concept of itinerant crime groups for a moment and, more broadly, discusses the concept of mobile – outbound, as we call it – offending patterns. These patterns are examined in two ways. First a descriptive and bivariate analysis of outbound property offences is executed. In this part of the chapter we aim to find out whether this crime pattern is worth further exploration and what its main features are. All outbound offender–offence pairs are considered. In the second part we explore possible explanations of outbound offending. As we particularly wish to focus on offenders who deliberately choose this offending pattern, we examine the behaviour of 'structural' outbound offenders who commit at least 90% of their crimes outside the district of Brussels, while residing in the city itself. The features of these offenders are briefly compared with the findings of the first part, after which a logistic regression is executed. Outbound offending being the dependent variable, we use a number of independent variables that recur throughout criminological literature as linked to mobility: maximisation of (expected) profits, risk reduction, ease of access, professionalism and co-offending.

[6] This chapter has been inspired by:
Van Daele, S., & Vander Beken, T. (2011). Outbound offending: the journey to crime and crime sprees. Journal of Environmental Psychology, 31(1), 70-78.

8.1 Local offending

Since the early 1980s, the criminology of place has gained a new momentum. Whereas traditional criminology tries to explain crime and deviant behaviour from various perspectives, environmental criminology does not question reasons for motivations, and instead assumes crime is rational behaviour (see Cornish & Clarke, 1986b). Criminal behaviour is therefore based on choice, although sometimes criminals are not totally aware of the choice they make (Canter & Youngs, 2008b, p. 14). By referring to routine activities theory, we observe the need for a motivated offender, in combination with a suitable target and the lack of capable guardians (Cohen & Felson, 1979, p. 588). We do not examine motivation itself, but instead we explore the convergence of these necessary precursors. Environmental criminology does not investigate why one person engages in criminal activity and another does not, but studies the environmental clues that facilitate criminal behaviour. As the location of the offence is six times more predictive for crime than the identity of the offender (Sherman, 1995, pp. 36-37), the criminology of place becomes an interesting domain for criminologists.

A number of criminologists focus on the issue of place and its possible crime facilitating or inhibiting factors (e.g. Brantingham & Brantingham, 1993b; Brown, 1982; Buettner & Spengler, 2001; Newman, 1976; Reynald & Elffers, 2009). Others, like ourselves, pay more attention to the converging process of perpetrator and target, which results in the study of criminal mobility. As this chapter focuses on offender mobility, it is the distance between offender residence and offence location that matters. Many crimes are committed in cities. Many persons – including offenders – live there and, through their population density, cities also provide large opportunity structures for crime to occur (Pyle, Hanten, Williams, Pearson, & Doyle, 1974, p. 34).

Crime trips into unknown territories are relatively rare (Van der Kemp & Van Koppen, 2007, p. 353). This has been observed both on the aggregate and on the individual level (Rengert et al., 1999). However, despite a traditional focus on local offending, a number of authors have pointed out that certain criminals do travel further. Morselli and Royer (2008) found offender mobility to be linked with criminal earnings, and encountered a number of highly mobile offenders. Because of their different approach, they do not calculate journey-to-crime in a traditional way. Thus, their observed mobility patterns appear less striking in relation to other studies. A careful reading of other studies reveals that a minority of offenders are indeed mobile. Patterns of mobile offenders have been observed and are often taken along in differentiated offender typologies. Herein, perpetrators offending in a circle around their homes are called marauders, whereas those travelling to other regions are referred to as commuters (Canter & Larkin, 1993; Kocsis et al., 2002; Meaney, 2004; Paulsen, 2007). Yet, mobile offenders too have incentives to leave known territory (Van Koppen & Jansen, 1998, p. 231).

Crime travelling is influenced by three main issues. First, expected profits, second, the expected risk and third, the ease with which the target can be reached (Bernasco & Luykx, 2003; Goodwill & Alison, 2006, p. 397; Steventon, 1996, p. 238). The ease with which a target can be reached is either an attraction – otherwise known as spatial attractiveness (Rhodes & Conly, 1981, p. 170) – or a barrier (Elffers, 2004, pp. 185-186). When targets are located nearby they become spatially attractive, and when they are not, they are subject to an additional barrier.

Guerry found that crimes against property were generally more common in towns than in rural areas, but he also acknowledged that enough exceptions exist to rule out a hasty conclusion (Phillips, 1972). Newton and Swoope (1987) distinguished mobile offenders from static ones. Maguire and Bennett found a close relationship between burglary rate and urbanisation. However, some wealthy towns prove to be interesting exceptions to this rule (Maguire & Bennett, 1982, pp. 19-20, p. 32). This offending pattern has been described as 'the search' (Bennett & Wright, 1984, p. 43; see also Rengert & Wasilchick, 1985, p. 66). Similar to this typology, Cromwell et al. (1991, p. 50) describe the 'journeyman' in their offender typology. Instead of coincidental convergence of offender and target, this typology is based on deliberately searching for criminal opportunities. This has been picked up again by Mawby, who described this phenomenon as 'rich pickings' (Mawby, 2001, p. 72). In a more recent study on Czech burglars, Polisenska (2008, p. 57) found that defining a crime as being committed close to home may be subject to perception (see also Brantingham & Brantingham, 1984b, p. 346). In other words, one criminal may consider a certain distance as 'far', while another sees the same trip as 'short'. She also found that some burglars travel further than we might expect. This differs from the strategy of most burglars, for whom burglary is a crime of opportunity and, as a result, they will be less likely to commit crimes in affluent areas (Bernasco, 2006, p. 152; Johnson & Bowers, 2004, p. 238; Malczewski & Poetz, 2005, pp. 516, 523; Van der Kemp & Van Koppen, 2007, p. 353).

Despite the fact that a number of authors have observed this type of offending, there has been limited interest in this crime pattern and most research focuses on local offending. This may partly be due to the fact that travelling to commit a crime is more the exception than the rule, but other issues may play a role as well. Mobility can sometimes be wrongly attributed if the anchor point of the offender is wrongly identified (Wiles & Costello, 2000, p. 35), or if there is no fixed anchor point at all (Rossmo, 2000), making it more difficult to assess criminal travelling and distinguish it from routine mobility. Also, much travel associated with crime is not primarily driven by criminal intentions and occurs towards regions that have strong connections with cities (Wiles & Costello, 2000, pp. 43-44). Through these connections, directional bias plays a role next to travelled distances (Costanzo et al., 1986; Rengert, 2004).

8.2 Data, method and backcloth

This chapter studies offenders who will travel to commit a crime despite the extra effort it entails, and attempts to identify what makes crime travelling worthwhile. It analyses these mobile offenders, but aims at a certain degree of generalisation and quantification. Hence, the analysis goes further than the study of itinerant crime groups which are considered in the rest of the book. We focus on mobility rather than affluence, and this forms the basis of data selection. However, we acknowledge that those travelling to affluent locations will probably make up a substantial part of the analysis. We consider outbound offending where the criminal lives in a city, and has sufficient crime opportunities near home but does not offend there. This analysis is applied to the district of Brussels. We examine the relation between outbound offending and a number of elements that are found in literature to correlate with target selection and high offender mobility. The following research questions are addressed in this chapter:

1. What is the proportion of outbound offending?

Many research papers on crime and mobility limit themselves to studying intra-city crime travelling; we want to know what proportion of crime trips that start in cities are neglected by this approach.

2. What elements favour outbound offending?

Cities provide great opportunities for crime: they provide a large concentration of potential targets and offer a great level of anonymity. What advantages do other areas have to make offenders leave this attractive crime setting and head somewhere else to commit offences? In order to answer these questions, we first provide descriptive statistics, followed by bivariate statistics. Finally, a logistic regression is executed.

As with the previous chapter, the analysed data refer to all serious property crimes in Belgium with known offenders for the period 2002–2006. We want to eliminate any errors in identifying anchor points as much as possible (see Wiles & Costello, 2000, pp. 40, 45), though we realise some mistakes are inevitable.

While home is often considered the normal anchor point, two main difficulties arise. First, multiple residences are registered for some offenders in the database, and it is impossible to determine their precise residence at the time of the offence. Thus, offenders with multiple residences are excluded from the analysis. Second, residential mobility is only one reason why anchor points might be wrongly identified. Other anchor points may be as important to the criminal as their residence (Bruinsma, 2007, p. 485), with the result that their starting points for criminal activity may vary. We reduce this bias in two stages, because we want to identify as many 'structural' outbound offenders as possible. First, only offenders who had committed five or more offences are taken into account. This excludes offenders who have committed one or two property crimes but have not become regular property criminals. Second, we class offenders as structural outbound offenders when they have committed at least 90% of their crimes outside the Brussels district. In this way, we exclude any offenders who show a mixed pattern of offending. For example, 15 offences can be attributed to offender A. As he has committed more than five offences, he falls within the first scope of analysis. However, he will only be considered a structural outbound offender if he has committed 90% of his crimes (in this case at least 14 out of 15) outside the Brussels district, meaning he could only have committed a maximum of one crime within the Brussels district.

The result is a dataset of 735 offenders who have committed five or more offences and live in the Brussels district, with only one registered residence. They have committed 5,500 offences, which leads to 6946 offender–offence pairs. One should take into account that only solved crimes are considered as the offenders are known. This might well influence observed mobility patterns. Some authors have formulated the hypothesis that mobile offenders are less likely to get caught than local offenders (Eck & Weisburd, 1995, p. 16; McIver, 1981, p. 43). As a consequence, our results underestimate the proportion of mobile offenders.

We then consider a number of offender and crime location features, which are derived from criminological literature and indicate higher mobility. Crime location characteristics are measured at municipality level. Although this can be criticised for not being a small unit of analysis (Oberwittler & Wikström, 2009), one should realise that crimes in the whole region of Belgium are considered, and thus, our area of research is still divided in 589 units. Furthermore, for mobile offending, decisions may be based on general perceptions about target areas, as it is less likely that offenders know the area in detail beforehand (Bernasco & Elffers, 2010). As such, municipalities provide a suitable level of analysis for our research.

- Wealth of target areas: Following previous research, referred to by some as 'rich pickings' (Mawby, 2001, p. 72), we would expect outbound offenders to head for more affluent areas. The 'wealth' of each area was assessed using a 'affluence index', that is designed by the National Institute for Statistics and uses values such as mean income and housing value to categorise it. The mean index for Belgium is 100, so every municipality with an affluence index over 100 is classed as wealthy. We also take into account the ratio between the target area affluence value and the criminal's residence area affluence value; the level of wealth in their own community may influence a criminal's perceptions of the affluence of other regions.
- Co-offending: Two or more criminals carrying out a crime together do not commit their crimes at the geographical mid-point between where they live. On the contrary, they are likely to offend near the anchor point of at least one group member (Bernasco, 2006, p. 147). Thus, offenders whose companions live outside the Brussels district may be likely to operate outside the district as well.
- Professionalism: as offenders learn from their previous crimes, they become more professional over time (Van Koppen & Jansen, 1998, p. 234). In addition, a certain degree of professionalism increases the range of operation (Barker, 2000, pp. 65-66).
- Accessibility of targets: some targets are more easily accessible than others. Accessibility is affected both by distance and by the transport system (Rephann, 1999, p. 373). The more escape routes there are from a potential target, the higher its chances of being victimised (Hakim et al., 2000, p. 12). For mobile offending, the use of motorways drastically reduces travel time to the target area (Fink, 1969; Laukkanen et al., 2008, p. 232; Maguire & Bennett, 1982, pp. 41-42; Rossmo, 2000, pp. 190, 214). In our sample, we use a two-step approach. First, we considered the proximity of motorways to the criminal's home. Second, we considered whether criminals use their most obvious route out of the city – the motorway that would take them out of the Brussels district as soon as possible. Not all criminals travel by car and are thus able to use motorways. Yet, these motorways run largely parallel with the main public transport lines, as such symbolising all major transport paths.
- Success rate: the risk of detection also plays a role in selection of target area (Bernasco & Luykx, 2003, p. 986). Therefore, criminals may be willing to travel further if the risks of detection are lower in the more distant area (Lu, 2003, p. 423). We conceptualise 'risk' in its most basic sense here – the

chances of arrest, which can be measured by comparing the number of offences without known offenders, with the total number of offences in each area. This measure is rather abstract, yet it is nevertheless objective.

- Criminal earnings: as criminals are more concerned with the rewards than the relative risks of their undertaking (Hakim, Rengert, & Shachmurove, 2001, pp. 134-135), earnings are expected to be at least as important as differences in success rate. Where criminals travel further to commit a crime, the rewards are often higher as well (Morselli & Royer, 2008), and thus further offences tend to net a greater return (Rhodes & Conly, 1981, p. 167). Unfortunately, our dataset provided no information on criminal earnings. We therefore used an alternative measure of those who committed two crimes or more at locations that are closer to each other than to the criminals' residence, within a period of eight hours. This meant that they did not have to travel home between crimes. This suggests that, although the earnings rise by committing more offences, the costs stay more or less fixed.

Although often used as a dependent or independent variable, we only consider distance in our descriptive analysis. The reason for this is twofold. First, distances will mostly be smaller for inbound offences, as the theoretical maximum distance is about 11km for offenders staying within the Brussels district. Second, we agree with Groff and McEwen (2006, p. 43) when they state that other, qualitative aspects may reveal more information than strict travel distance does.

Our analysis uses offender–offence pairs to describe outbound offending in general. The use of these pairs is not new (also see Bernasco & Block, 2009; Hodgson & Costello, 2006; Kleemans, 1996). We first consider outbound offending in general, i.e. all offender–offence pairs that start within Brussels and end somewhere else. In order to focus on structural outbound offending, we then examine those outbound offences committed by offenders who travel beyond Brussels to commit at least 90% of their crimes. We use the individual offender as unit of analysis, and distinguish structural outbound offenders from the rest. As two-thirds of journey-to-crime variation is situated on the offender level (Smith et al., 2009, p. 232), we believe this approach to be suitable. Moreover, this analysis focuses on those offenders for whom outbound offending is a structural element of their criminal behaviour and therefore focuses on deliberate (though perhaps subconscious) motivations for outbound offending.

The district of Brussels consists of 19 municipalities (one of them being the municipality of Brussels). The borders between these areas are mainly administrative: Brussels can be considered as one city, and its various entities are not clearly distinguishable. We acknowledge these borders are not constructed for purposes of research designs (Weisburd et al., 2009, pp. 19-20). However, given the available information on municipality level and the focus on mobile offending, we believe analyses at municipality level to be sufficient.

The Brussels district, the capital of Belgium, has just over 1 million inhabitants spread over 161.4km^2. The population density varies between 1,869.8 inhabitants per km^2 and 21,622.7 inhabitants per km^2. Each area has been awarded an affluence index, for which the Belgian average is 100. Within the district of Brussels, these indexes range from 51.8 to 113.8. Seven areas have an affluence index above the average. Thus, even within the Brussels district, a large variation exists. The district is surrounded by a motorway ring road, so it is easy to reach the motorway from any part of Brussels. The southern part of the city is the only area where the ring road is located further away from the city. Moreover, a number of important motorways come together at the Brussels ring road, allowing easy access to the rest of Belgium.

In the neighbourhoods where these motorways reach Brussels, people may tend to travel in a particular direction. Ten of the 19 areas are located near to these motorway nodes. Four areas (Ganshoren, Sint-Agatha-Berchem, Koekelberg and Sint-Jans-Molenbeek) are located in the north-west, and people there have an easy route towards Ghent and the Belgian coast on the E 40 motorway. Residents of one municipality, Brussels itself, tend to travel towards Antwerp, either on the A12 or the E19 (which are parallel roads, one is an old main road, the other a newer motorway). People from three areas (Evere, Schaarbeek, Sint-Lambrechts-Woluwe) can easily travel eastward towards Liège on the E40, and those from Watermaal-Bosvoorde and Oudergem can travel south-east, in the direction of Namur and Luxemburg.

8.3 Outbound offending in general

Offenders living in Brussels are responsible for 6,946 offender–offence pairs. As the offender–offence pairs are used, these outbound offences are both committed by structural outbound offenders and occasional outbound offenders (for which outbound crimes make up less than 90% of their offences). Of these pairs:

- 3,372 (48.5%) are 'outbound' – crime trips that started in the district of Brussels and end outside it. Of these, 447 (13.3%) trips end in a area adjoining the Brussels district.

- 2,111 (30.4%) are subject to mobility within the Brussels district – i.e. the offender travels outside his area of residence but stays within the district.
- 1,463 (21.1%) are local – the offender does not leave his own area to commit his crime.

It is clear from this that outbound offending makes up a substantial proportion of the data set of serious property crimes, and is therefore worth exploring further. Even if we eliminate crime trips to adjoining areas, over 42% (2,925 crimes) of all these crimes can be classed as outbound offences.

The term 'rich pickings' is apposite in many cases – the target areas of outbound offenders have a mean affluence index of 106.9, compared with 82.0 for the non-outbound offences. Outbound offences start in areas with a mean affluence index of 76.1, compared with 76.7 for the other offenders. Thus, although their anchor points do not differ drastically, their target areas do. It is possible to target affluent areas within the Brussels district, but offenders that commit crimes in their local areas appear less likely to do so than the outbound offenders.

In general, mobility positively correlates with the wealth of the target's neighbourhood ($r=0.28$; $p<0.01$). However, when we consider only outbound offences, we observe a negative correlation of $r=-0.60$ ($p<0.01$). Thus, it appears that outbound offenders are likely to look for affluent regions in the more immediate surroundings of their anchor point, and if they travel further they have other reasons to do so. This applies to both structural ($r=-0.43$; $p<0.01$) and other ($r=-0.58$; $p<0.01$) outbound offenders.

One possibility may be that these offenders travel further because they start their crime trips near the anchor points of any accomplices. Some 76.2% of the outbound offender–offence pairs are committed with others, whereas this is the case for 'only' 56.5% of the pairs within the Brussels district. Thus, outbound offending is more likely to be the work of several people at a time ($Chi^2=300.0$; $df=1$; $p<0.01$). However, this only reveals that co-offending is linked with outbound offending (Cramer's $V=0.208$; $p<0.01$); it does not reveal any information on the anchor point of the accomplices. The next question, therefore is whether the accomplices are likely to live outside the district or not. For co-offending, 66.9% of outbound offenders have accomplices who do not reside in the Brussels district, meaning their residence is located outside the district or is unknown. For offences within the district of Brussels, this is even higher, at 69.7% ($Chi^2 = 4.0$; $df=1$; $p<.05$). Thus, although co-offenders appear to be more likely to travel to commit their crimes, there is no clear evidence that this is caused by their companions living outside the district.

We first measure 'professionalism' by the total number of offences committed, and find that outbound offender–offence pairs are more likely to have a professional/experienced offender involved (27.52 crimes per offender on average) than other pairs (9.59 crimes per offender on average). Travelled distance is correlated with number of offences ($r=0.287$; $p<0.01$). This mainly reflects the differences between outbound and within-district offending, but shows no strong correlation within each group ($r=0.06$; $p<0.01$ for within-district pairs; $r=-0.03$; $p=0.05$ for outbound offending pairs). As we only include offenders who had committed five or more offences in our analysis, the correlation between the number of crimes and the distance travelled to commit them may explain why we find such a large proportion of outbound offending in the first place.

Special attention is given to accessibility of the target areas. As the effort put into travelling to the crime is higher for outbound offending than for offences committed within the Brussels district, we would expect offenders to compensate for these efforts by using more effective means of transport. Motorways cross nearly half of all Belgian municipalities (288 out of 589; or 48.9%). Thus, if the crimes are equally spread, fewer than half would be expected to be committed in such an area. However, 75.4% of outbound offences are committed in these areas. Outbound offenders are therefore likely to use motorways as a more effective way of transport.

Whether they are as likely to use the same motorway as their starting point (i.e. as the fastest way to get out of Brussels) is less certain. Only in 13.2% of the outbound offending cases (26.6% of the outbound offences located near a motorway) is the motorway that is nearest to their target the same as the motorway that is situated closest to the area where they live. Thus, although motorways do function as a more effective means of transport, they are not necessarily used to leave the home district as soon as possible.

Success rates, or the risks of detection, are also looked at. Travelling increases the effort needed to commit a crime, and thus leads to higher costs. Higher earnings might compensate for the cost of travel, and committing a crime in an area where the risk of arrest is reduced (which is more expensive to the criminal than a few extra litres of petrol) would certainly seem to. Thus, if mobile offenders have more success (lower levels of detection), the effort they have put in to get there could be worthwhile. However, we find that while outbound offenders have a success rate of 0.90, for offenders who stay within the district of Brussels this increases to 0.97.

A final element is serial offending, which we use as an alternative measure for criminal earnings. For offences within Brussels, 12.1% formed part of a crime spree (crimes committed within 8 hours of each other). For offences by outbound offenders, 41.8% were part of a crime spree. This figure overrates the true level of serial offending, as it also includes offences as series when various acts can in fact be considered as one crime, for example a burglar breaking into a garden house to take a ladder, which then he uses to break into the house. However, even if we exclude these offences outbound offending still includes 28.7% serial offending, compared with only 6.1% for offending within Brussels. Thus, outbound offenders are four times more likely to operate in sprees and reduce the extra costs by committing several crimes. Serial offending is also more likely to occur in affluent areas (36.8% series) than in poorer areas (17.5% series).

Thus outbound offending is likely to occur at targets that are wealthy, to be carried out by more experienced offenders and co-offenders, to form part of a crime series and to be located near motorways. However, this does not mean that outbound offending involves features that would offset the effort of travelling. Within outbound offences, wealth and travelled distance are inversely correlated. Co-offending does not explain outbound offending such that offences would be committed near the anchor point of another offender. Although motorways are used, they are not necessarily those motorways that provide the quickest exit from Brussels. Finally, the chances of success do not seem to play a major role, as the chosen target areas have lower success rates than the more immediate environment has.

8.4 Structural outbound offending

Some 128 of 735 offenders are structural outbound offenders and responsible for 2178 offender–offence pairs. We will use the previously described measures to explore whether there are any substantial differences between structural outbound offending and occasional outbound offending.

The average affluence rate of regions targeted by structural offenders is comparable with that of occasional outbound offenders: 107.5 (107.2 if we take into account all offences of this offender group) versus 106.9. They do seem to travel a little further, as only 8.0% of their outbound offences are committed in a municipality adjacent to Brussels, compared with 13.3% for outbound offending in general.

In total, 81.3% of their outbound offences were committed by two or more offenders. These offenders have committed 17.0 offences on average (the individual offender is our unit of analysis for this calculation). Some 72.2% of offenders commit their crime near a motorway, and for 14.4% of offenders this motorway is the same as the one they live close to. The average success rate for the areas they operate in is 0.89, and 51.7% of their offences form part of a series of offences.

Offenders who commit outbound offences in a structural way do not follow any fundamentally different patterns than occasional outbound offenders. It is true that they travel slightly further, commit more offences on average, are more likely to stay near the motorways, are more likely to operate in series and even manage to target areas where they are more successful. However, the differences compared to general outbound offending are quite modest. No additional element can be found in the data set to indicate why structural outbound offenders favour outbound offending.

Our next step is to execute a binary logistic regression. Here, we consider structural outbound offending at the level of the individual offender. As each offender has one residence (those with multiple residences have been excluded from analysis), offender and residence features are easy to calculate. For the other variables – which were target and offence related – we use the percentages of crimes that are committed within a region that is affluent or not, successful or not, and so on. This results in some loss of information, because a range of values is replaced by just one central value. As we are attempting to explain the general tendencies of offenders – factors that make an offender (nearly) always head for targets outside the home area – we believe that the loss of information is not significant. Moreover, despite the confined loss of information, the main advantage of this approach is that it weighs all offenders as equal and therefore does not overestimate the patterns of multiple offenders. What this model therefore explains is the odds of an offender becoming a structural outbound offender. We divide these features into four groups. First we look at the wealth of a target area, because we observed large differences in target area affluence between outbound offending and offending within the Brussels district. Second, we look at features relating to success, as we would expect offenders to operate in regions they think of as 'safe' (from arrest). Third, we study accessibility as measured by motorways, and finally some additional background features are taken into account.

The result of this regression is shown in Table 8.1. The Hosmer and Lemeshow test is not significant, the model thus showing a good fit (Chi^2=2167; df=8; p=0.98). The relative R^2 of Cox and Snell (0.45) and Nagelkerke (0.75) show that the model explains a substantial part of the encountered variation, resulting in an overall correctly predicted percentage of 93.9%.

Table 8.1: Logistic regression of structural outbound offending

	B	S.E.	Wald	df	Sig.	Exp(B)	95% C.I.for EXP(B)	
							Lower	Upper
% affluent target areas	1.75	.54	10.47	1	.00	5.78	2.00	16.71
Affluent residence area	–.50	.61	.67	1	.41	.61	.18	2.01
% high success target areas	–5.64	.57	97.68	1	.00	.004	.001	.01
High success residence area	–.39	.62	.39	1	.53	.68	.20	2.30
% target areas near motorways	2.13	.68	9.99	1	.00	8.44	2.25	31.66
Residence area near motorways	–.96	.43	4.92	1	.03	.38	.16	.89
% near same motorway	–3.33	.84	15.61	1	.00	.04	.01	.18
Number of crimes	.05	.02	5.57	1	.02	1.05	1.01	1.10
% of co-offended crimes	.96	.58	2.74	1	.10	2.60	.84	8.07
% of crimes in series	3.06	.73	17.68	1	.00	21.40	5.13	89.26
Constant	–1.14	1.18	.93	1	.34	.32		

The largest positive effects are found for affluent target areas, target areas that were located near motorways and the number of crimes being committed in series. The largest negative effects are found for success rate of the target areas and the target and residence being located near the same motorway. For co-offending and features of the area of residence, effects are less or not significant.

8.5 Implications

The aim of the study is to assess the influence of the environmental setting on outbound offending, focusing on offenders who are rather atypical in their criminal behaviour. Although there is a large variation in levels of wealth in different areas of Brussels, we only find small differences in the wealth of areas where criminals who operate locally live, and the neighbourhoods of those who are outbound offenders. This has been extended in our binary logistic regression. Offenders are not more likely to become structural outbound offenders when they live in poor areas or areas with a low success rate. In fact, the features of their home region are irrelevant to determine outbound offending. The 'criminal opportunity' perspective (see Cohen & Felson, 1981) therefore fits best. This was to be expected, because the measures we use are developed for use in opportunity structures (Bernasco & Luykx, 2003; Goodwill & Alison, 2006; Steventon, 1996).

Success has a negative effect on the likelihood of criminals leaving the Brussels district to commit crimes. On the contrary, if offenders would want to operate in areas where the chances of arrests are lower, they would not have to travel far at all. Two issues are taken into account. First, we calculate the success rate in its most objective way – i.e. the chances of arrest in a certain area. It is unlikely that offenders can make this judgement for themselves very easily. Any perceptions they have about their chances of success are more likely to be subjective than objective (Matsueda, Kraeger, & Huizinga, 2006).

Furthermore, previous research has demonstrated that offenders are more likely to make changes when choosing their actual target than they are in deciding on the target area generally (Tillyer & Kennedy, 2008, pp. 76-77). This brings us to the second issue: our level of analysis. It has been noted by Rengert and Wasilchick (1985) that offenders first head for a target area, and look for a suitable target once they arrive. Rengert and Wasilchick (1985, p. 55) called this the search space, of which the space where the criminal activity occurs is only a subset. Other authors have made this distinction as well (Bernasco & Luykx, 2003, p. 986; Cornish & Clarke, 1986a, pp. 3-5). In this chapter we look at mobile offenders, who, it is assumed, would need to make the initial step of selecting a suitable area more deliberately. Taking into account the findings from other researchers that offenders pay more attention to the expected profits than to the risks they take (Hakim et al., 2001, pp. 134-135) , and that criminals base their perceived likelihood of success more on the features of the individual target, rather than the wider area's perceived likelihood of success (see above), attractiveness can be expected to play a more crucial role than an area's success rate does.

We do observe a negative correlation between success rate and the affluence of target areas ($r=-0.34$; $p<0.01$). Therefore, the negative effect of the success rate may be linked to the importance of affluence over success. Yet, one has to be aware that success rates can also be influenced by differences in reporting rates between urban and rural areas.

Structural outbound offenders are more likely to commit crimes near motorways than other offenders. This confirms the expectation that outbound offending and the costs this brings are compensated by using efficient transport routes.

However, this does not mean that outbound offenders also live near motorways, and when the criminal's residence and his target are located near the same motorway, the chances for structural outbound offending substantially decrease. Nevertheless, it is important to take into account that offenders operating in the same area as their residence have no need to use the motorway; thus, the odds of a criminal using the motorway near to his residence are biased by this measure.

Carrying out several offences in a short space of time has a large positive effect on the odds ratio and is linked to structural outbound offending. Although we use this as an alternative measure to estimate earnings, it is also possible that this is another example of a more effective means of transport. If one only travels a route once to commit three offences, one can travel three times as far and still be as efficient, even if we only consider travel time and costs. Additionally, the risks of apprehension during travel, crossing of physical (Elffers, 2004) and social borders (Reynald et al., 2008) and planning activities (Johnson & Bowers, 2004, p. 243) are also divided by three, and at a later stage storage and selling efforts per crime become lower as well. As such, the benefits of spree offending may be greater than expected, and may make it a lucrative and worthwhile approach.

The analysis does not control for opportunity structure by means of population density (see Pyle et al., 1974). We do acknowledge that opportunity structure certainly plays a role in offending patterns. Yet, implementing it here would enclose a major flaw. If the patterns of the studied offenders would be largely influenced by opportunity structures, they would have had no reason at all to travel outbound. After all, they live within such a major opportunity structure. A t-test shows that offenders in our sample not being considered structural outbound offenders – for they have committed less than 90% of their crimes outside Brussels – commit their crimes in areas with an average of 7,022.26 persons/km^2, while this is only 823.27 persons/km^2 for structural outbound offenders. Thus, offending outside Brussels in itself makes opportunity structures less important. Yet, future work could elaborate on the role of opportunity structures within the pattern of outbound offending.

Our data does not allow us to differentiate between type of offence. Thus, we are unable to define whether outbound offending is the result of particular crime attractors (see for example Wiles & Costello, 2000, p. 46). Yet, we believe the effect of these attractors in our analysis to be negligible. First, outbound offenders travel 41.99km on average (even 45.41km if we consider each individual crime). As this distance is quite large, chances are low that particular small-scale attractors such as shopping malls would play a major role over these distances. Only larger attractors could play, for example the seaside which can be considered a large leisure area. In Figure 8.1, we have drawn a scatterplot of all outbound offences encountered in our sample in relation to the distance to Brussels. It shows indeed that the seaside (indicated on the top left) is a common area for outbound offenders. This suggests what Wiles and Costello (2000, p. 43) stated, namely that crime travelling often has no deviant intentions in the first place. Next to the seaside, however, we notice outbound offences being equally spread around Brussels. As such, except for the seaside, no particular crime attractors are observed at the macro-level.

Figure 8.1: Outbound offending map

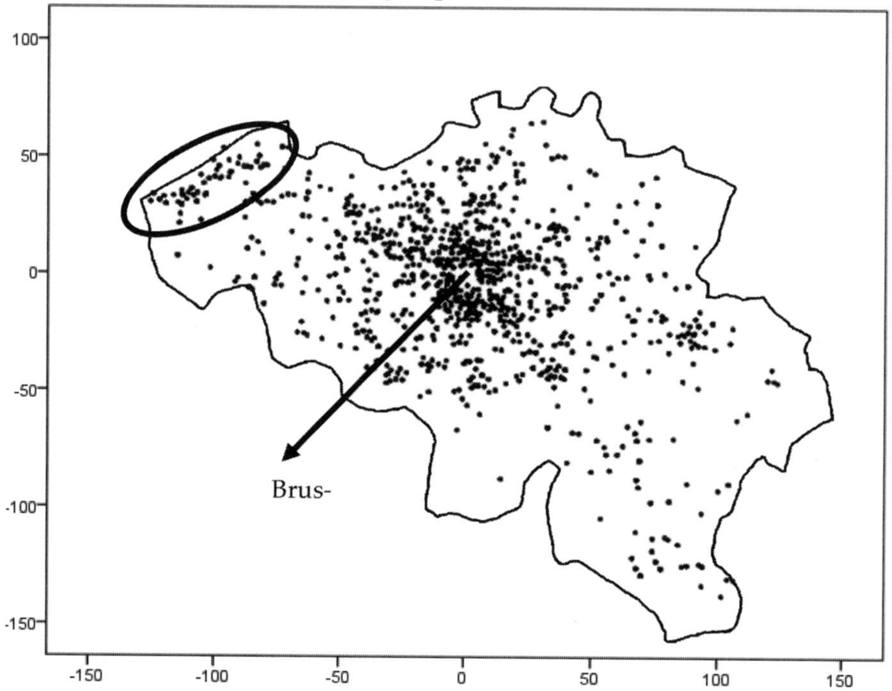

By focusing on outbound offending this chapter examines an often-neglected offending pattern. It uses a number of area indicators. Although previous researchers have mentioned such offending as a typology in ethnographic research (see above), this chapter links them with opportunity-related variables. Outbound offending can be considered criminal commuting and shows that criminal commuters, although often travelling towards opportunity structures, may sometimes choose to do otherwise.

A number of future improvements could be made. This chapter uses data at the municipality level. As outbound offending involves travelling to new areas, these data are sufficient to reveal substantial differences. Nevertheless, future research could elaborate further using neighbourhood-level data and/or characteristics of the individual targets. This approach would allow us to study the changing role of certain levels of analysis as distances increase.

Another step could be to elaborate further the role of short-term serial offending, investigating which issues play an important role, what the advantages and disadvantages of such an offending pattern are, or how this influences crime travelling in general, independent of whether this travelling occurs towards or from cities. Although offending sprees have been used in this chapter as an alternative measure for earnings, it could also be studied in itself. The same can be said for the use of motorways. While we used the proximity of motorways to measure accessibility, the role of motorways or other means of transport could provide useful information in the study of criminal mobility.

8.6 Conclusion

In this chapter, we examined outbound offending, or crime trips that start in a city but have a target outside that city. Because of the distances involved, we considered data at municipality level. Although most studies focus on intra-city offending, we observed that nearly half of the crime trips that started in the district of Brussels were outbound, indicating these often-neglected crime trips are worth examining. Even if we exclude those trips that ended in areas adjoining the Brussels district, over 40% of the crime trips still involved outward travel.

The term 'rich pickings', previously used to describe this type of offending, appears to be appropriate as this type of offence is consistently targeted at more affluent areas. In order to eliminate any coincidental outbound crimes, for example due to a short stay with friends/family outside the district, we further focused on those offenders for whom outbound offending was a structural characteristic (i.e. 90% or more of their crimes were committed outside the Brussels district). We found the wealth of the target areas was an important indication, but other issues played a role as well. The feature that appeared to have the greatest impact was that of offending in series, which does not belong to either one of the three characteristics mentioned in previous literature and was used by us an alternative indication for criminal earnings. A follow-on question is, therefore, how serial offending contributes to travelling – should we view it as a redistribution of travel costs or a multiplication of earnings per trip, or is it merely a indicator of the higher professionalism of these offenders and offender groups?

Co-offending was highly likely among outbound offenders, though this could not be attributed to crimes being committed near the residence of the other offender. Thus, although offender groups are likely to travel further, our findings do not confirm that this is linked to the different anchor points of the group members. More important, perhaps, was the fact that offences were more likely to be committed at locations near large motorways. Thus, next to affluence, accessibility plays a role in outbound offenders' choice of a target. This is congruent with what we expected from previous research. However, we found that success had no positive effect on the odds for outbound offending. Whilst this may partly be due to our objective measure of success – which takes no account of a criminal's subjective perceptions about individual targets – it is surprising that it is completely subordinate to the attractiveness and accessibility of the target.

While offending patterns are often studied within cities, this chapter shows structural outbound offending patterns to be worthy of study. Moreover, even this large proportion may underestimate mobile offending, as our data involved solved crimes and mobile offenders are expected to be caught less. If this is the case, mobile offending patterns may be as common as intra-city crime trips, standing up for more research on these rarely examined patterns.

In addition to making up a large proportion of outbound crime trips in general, the offending pattern appears to work to a different logic to near-home offending: profit maximisation and travel effectiveness are priorities, rather than cost and travel minimisation. Neglecting to study these trips means this difference is missed, as is the possibility that offenders may use very different ways of reasoning and still be considered rational offenders. In sum, there is more variety in offending pattern principles than is often assumed.

Chapter 9. Explaining offender mobility of itinerant crime groups[7]

Throughout the book, we have demonstrated that itinerant crime groups are highly mobile. This is reflected in larger travelled distances and a different distance decay curve. Observing this is one thing, explaining another. We have noticed that the mobility cannot be explained by a wrong conception of the anchor point and that outbound offending in general is related to various elements, target affluence and spree offending being the most important ones. In this chapter, we further explore the explanations of these offenders' mobility. Although we do consider some quantifiable elements such as the affluence of their target regions, we provide some deeper insights in the operations of these groups and subsequently, even consider the mobility from the offenders' perspective.

9.1 Target oriented explanations

A first possibility to find explanations for certain patterns is looking at the targets that are chosen. According to Bernasco en Luykx (2003) this refers to three main aspects. The first is attractiveness, which refers to expected profits. Second, opportunity deals with the perceived risk. Finally, accessibility considers the ease with which the target can be reached.

Attractiveness of targets aimed at by itinerant crime groups is split into two aspects. On the level of target choice, itinerant crime groups tend to go less for commercial targets (45% of the targets are dwellings) than other offenders (only 13.6% dwellings). As commercial targets are expected to be more profitable and high gains are correlated to high mobility (Morselli & Royer, 2008), itinerant crime groups do not compensate for their crime travelling by earning more profits.

[7] The part of this chapter that uses the information coming from offender interviews, has been inspired by:
Van Daele, S., & Vander Beken, T. (in press). Out of sight, out of mind? Awareness space and mobile offenders. European Journal of Crime, Criminal Law and Criminal Justice.

On a higher geographical level, however, attractiveness does affect target choice. Each Belgian communality has been attributed a welfare-index, based on the average income. In general, property crimes are mostly committed in relatively poor towns and cities (average welfare-index 96.8), while itinerant crime groups tend to commit their crimes in richer areas (welfare-index 104.8). However, these itinerant crime groups mainly live in poorer areas (welfare-index 88.4) than other offenders do (welfare-index 94.5). Thus, although the crimes committed by itinerant crime groups are not the most profitable ones, they do target rich areas.

In order to measure opportunity, we divided the number of crimes in our sample (these are the crimes for which the offender is known) by the total number of serious property crimes for each communality. In this way, opportunity is measured in a pure sense, by calculating the chances of walking away after the crime. Strange enough, itinerant crime groups do not commit their crimes in successful areas: their mean success rate is 0.89 while it is 0.91 for other offenders. What is observed, however, is that these groups commit more crimes in rural areas, the average population density being 705.0 persons per square kilometre, versus 2029.7 for other offenders. Although the success rate in these areas is lower, offenders may perceive otherwise, because there are less people around. In order to confirm this, however, more information on motivational aspects of offenders is needed.

A final issue in target related explanations refers to accessibility. It is argued that offenders aim mostly for those targets which are easily accessible. If this is the case on a local level, why would it not be so on national level? Fink (1969) found that external offenders commit most of their crimes near major highways, in this way keeping the risk of accessing an unknown region within certain boundaries. Elffers (2004) discusses the barriers on the journey to crime. He pays attention to rivers and landmarks, but on larger scale, this will only play a minor role. Next to inhibiting barriers, there might as well be facilitating factors, compensating for these barriers. The most visual are arterial roads, particularly motorways. In a number of cases, the use of motorways has been observed: offenders driving over 100 km, committing a couple of burglaries and returning afterwards, proven by tracing the extensive cell phone traffic. Remarkable is the fact that this is not confirmed in our database as an explanatory issue. Yes, itinerant crime groups commit their crimes near motorways (68.7%), but this is even more the case for other offenders (75.4%).

The offender interviews draw a similar picture, although some differences do exist. Despite their high mobility, respondents claimed to choose their targets based on similar elements to those observed in other research. This was the case even for the most mobile burglars. They chose against burgling houses where the residents were present and were deterred by dogs and alarms. They preferred easy-to-enter houses that were a bit secluded, mirroring the findings of other research using offender interviews in Belgium (Verwee et al., 2007).

Other elements were less obvious. Some offenders went for rich-looking houses because they expected more profits. Yet, two offenders deliberately did the opposite, pointing out that the looks of a house tell little about what can be found inside. Moreover, rich houses are more likely to have alarms, according to the interviewees.

> *"[...] And if you're unlucky, they shoot at your head too"*

As for target choice, both risk perception and opportunity play a role. In that sense, these offenders do not differ dramatically from other offenders.

The offenders mainly involved in residential burglaries explicitly mentioned operating outside the cities where they stayed. Some of them operated in one or two regions, others admitted to having committed crimes all over the country:

> *"We had not planned where to go. We left at dusk and started to offend when it was completely dark. [...] I never had a feeling of recognition. I might have been to the same district, but as far as I know not in the same neighbourhood, let alone the same house"*

These offenders used the main Belgian traffic lines for travelling. They sometimes travelled by train, but more often used cars to reach their targets. This gave them opportunities to carry more loot and offered more freedom to travel. They regularly used motorways, but this did not necessarily mean their target was located near these roads. Using motorways to leave their home regions, it was highly possible that they would travel several kilometres in search for a target after leaving the motorway:

> *"Yes, we used the motorway, but this does not mean we offended nearby that motorway. It often occurred that we drove quite some time on other roads too."*

Therefore, although the use of motorways helps to understand the offenders' capacity for travelling, it cannot explain what made them choose to be mobile. After all, these facilities could be used by other offenders. We therefore wanted to investigate the rationale for travelling and did so through questions about target choice and awareness space.

Some target oriented observations seem to explain the mobile behaviour of itinerant crime groups: they target rich areas, rural areas and case file analysis shows the use of motorways. However, these types of explanations is insufficient for several reasons. First, it is unclear why rural areas would be targeted, because they are not characterised by higher success rates. Second, highways appear to be used by other offenders as well. Although this is able to explain mobility, it does not explain the differences between mobility of itinerant crime groups and other offenders. And third, this can be said for all target oriented features: they are not different for other offenders. Why would other offenders engage less in 'rich pickings' and stay more within their own neighbourhood? Therefore, explanations from another perspective are investigated as well: from the point of the offender.

9.2 Offender oriented results

Not only target features may influence the criminal trip. Offender related issues play a role as well. In this perspective, three main issues are dealt with: offender features, anchor point and awareness space. Members of 'itinerant crime groups' are slightly older than other offenders, but the difference is fractional and not significant. Case files show that most offenders are rather young or middle-aged. Several groups contain older offenders born in the 1950s or even the 1940s. A slightly larger proportion is born in the 1960s. The vast majority of nearly all itinerant crime groups are perpetrators born in the 1970s and the first half of the 1980s. Most offenders are in their twenties or thirties. Several groups contain older offenders as well.

Most offenders are experienced too. As a minimum of ten crimes has been set as a condition, all offenders are experienced. But there is more. They often already have a criminal record, either in their home country, in Belgium or even a third country. The crimes they have been known for mostly include property crimes, but also violence –whether or not while committing property crimes–, fraud, forgery and sometimes even drug crimes. While most offenders are adults and often experienced, this is not always the case. Two groups in our sample use minors for criminal purposes.

Itinerant crime groups are from Eastern European origin. As such, they can be considered as part of an ethnic minority. However, this forms no visible minority and, thus, constitutes no barrier for mobility. Several groups have no homogenous composition. Participating people come from all sorts of Eastern

European countries (Romania, former Yugoslavia, Albania, Ukraine, Bulgaria, Slovenia, Russia, Czech Republic, Belarus) to Western European offenders (French, Dutch, Belgian and naturalized Belgian) and even Southern European (Italian) and Northern African (Moroccan) offenders.

Perhaps with the exception of age for some of them, itinerant crime groups are experienced, not part of a truly visible ethnic minority and thus conform what Gabor and Gottheil (1984) found as features of mobile offenders. Yet, there should be more, because personal characteristics can be attributed to offender mobility, but cannot really explain it.

9.3 Linking offenders to targets: the role of awareness space

Brantingham and Brantingham (1981b) defined the awareness space as the area of which offenders have knowledge. The gaining of this knowledge is based on both criminal and neutral activities (Brantingham & Brantingham, 1981b, p. 35). Neutral activities can include work, school, shopping and leisure. However, one may wonder whether the importance of awareness space exists only in local offending. Does awareness space mainly indicates mobility restrictions or does it play a broader role? A large variation in offender mobility exists. Offenders that commit crimes near home may do so because they know the neighbourhood, but what does that say about offenders that travel far distances? Does this mean they have a larger awareness space? Or is it more, that these offences occur outside the offender's awareness space?

Our case file analysis reveals that, after the decision to commit housebreaking has been taken, there is often little or no further preparation. Bennett and Wright (1984, pp. 45-46) called this typology 'the search'. In their sample, nearly half of the offenders belong to this type. Other authors observed this typology as well, also in Belgium (see Verwee et al., 2007, pp. 104-106). Repeat victimization occurs regularly. Six groups hit the same targets during their operations. Another group does not really target the same premises, but always targets the same type of holiday homes, with exactly the same layout. For burglaries, repeat victimization is not an exclusive operation method of these groups. On the contrary, re-victimization is quite common (Nee & Meenaghan, 2006, p. 946). Itinerant crime groups follow no totally different preparation scheme than other burglars either.

Various risk reducing measures have been observed. One often encountered strategy is reconnaissance activity, noticed in 18 out of 27 case files. Most reconnaissance activities are performed shortly –one or a couple of days– before the criminal operations. Concerning housebreakings, reconnaissance is often limited to a rather short exploration of the area, not infrequently by other accomplices than those doing the burglary later on. For commercial burglaries, this is more systematic: more information is obtained and targets are picked more carefully. One group had inside information on their targets and another had a map with all companies of their target type in Belgium and France.

Using strategies such as repeat victimization, planning, reconnaissance and mapping, these offender groups become familiar with their target areas and become aware of the features of their region of operation. Despite some exceptions, no information on 'innocent creation of awareness space' is known for these groups. Repeat victimization by the same groups may be an explanation for further criminal activity, but it does not explain the initial criminal behaviour within a certain region. In general, crime trips into unknown territories are relatively rare (Palmer et al., 2002, p. 12; Van der Kemp & Van Koppen, 2007, p. 353). For the itinerant crime groups, reconnaissance activities and maps can function as awareness space generators. Nevertheless, as there is already some criminal intent involved, the composition of this awareness space emerges mostly not in an innocent way. Awareness space is therefore less straightforward as it is for other offenders.

The interviews give a slightly more different picture. However, one should not forget that most of the offenders were involved in residential burglaries and crime that require relatively little expertise. Furthermore, because of the voluntary participation of the interviewed offenders, it is quite likely that those taking part in rather organised criminal structures will refuse more often to take part in the research.

We explicitly asked how offenders came to choose certain offending regions. For the crimes that are committed near their residence, the answer is obvious. Yet, we also want to find out whether other chosen districts are also part of their awareness space. Two persons committed crimes while returning from an unsuccessful job searching trip. They had obtained some – incorrect – information on where they could find work and because they needed money, they chose to commit crimes on the way back home. Two other respondents knew someone from earlier days in another region and travelled there to meet them. It was only afterwards – and not necessarily in the company of the person living there – that they offended. Thus, these offenders encountered their target while travelling for non-criminal purposes. However, one can hardly assume they knew the region well after having only been there once. Therefore, despite the non-criminal nature of their trip, one cannot say the area where they offended in this case belonged to their awareness space:

> *"We saw the house while driving around through several districts and decided to instantly [offend]."*

Other offenders do travel with criminal intentions in mind. Several motives play a role here. Two offenders travelled because they planned to offend in wealthy areas, believing that operating outside the city would lead to higher profits. Three other offenders did not consider profits, paying more attention to risk instead. According to them, smaller municipalities have fewer police, which reduces the risk of arrest. Moreover, these areas contain more secluded houses, making it less likely to be seen. Operating in rural areas for them meant more privacy and, hence, a higher success rate:

> *"Not in [city X] because it's too crowded, busy, too much police. In smaller districts, when the police comes after you, you can still run into the fields or from garden to garden."*

Thus, five offenders made a deliberate choice either to attempt to maximise profit or reduce risk. However, choosing the actual area to offend was not based on earlier experience, but was mostly inspired by a number of rather abstract perceptions. Six other offenders did not make a clear choice, but drove around until a suitable target was spotted. If it turned out that residents were present or there were technical difficulties to enter, they chose another target. They were highly opportunistic and had difficulties remembering where precisely they had offended. One offender even indicated to be sometimes surprised on his way back, noticing how far he had travelled. These offenders' crime trips showed no clear patterns. Their spatial awareness of Belgium was also limited. They had little knowledge of where they had previously been or the locations of the various Belgian cities. One offender even mentioned travelling to the northern part of the country especially because he considered it wealthier. However, when we discussed the towns he visited, it turned out they were often located in the south. Thus, the offenders' spatial awareness often did not exceed a number of vague, abstract assumptions and opinions:

> *"The houses were a bit apart, we had the impression that residents were not there. When the house is apart, we don't draw the attention [...] Security measures were also important, so no visible alarms or high gates: houses that were quite accessible"*

We also find that offenders pay attention to either positive (expected profits) or negative (reduced risk) issues. Although we asked about other elements as well, there appears to be no combination among individual offenders. This may refine findings from studies on the aggregate level that observed both positive and negative elements to play a role in target location choice.

In fact we may divide the sample of interviewed offenders into three main groups. The first group operates within the vicinity of where they stay, which is often in hotels. These offenders soon get involved in crime, and had no time to develop an awareness space beforehand. They can be compared with the Sheffield persistent offenders as described by Bottoms and Wiles (2002). Due to their relatively short stay, they have no access to leisure activities and their routines were bound to a small area.

A second group operates both nearby and far away from the city where they live. Their travelling behaviour has more to do with their targets than with their awareness space: they operate in shopping centres, steal from particular shops or target people at cash dispensers. Because they do not want to operate in the same locations all the time, they expand their operation area to other regions.

The third and most remarkable group consists of offenders who deliberately choose to travel long distances. This is sometimes prompted by non-criminal travelling, for example, in search for work or meeting old friends, which does not allow us to describe it as a routine activity. Other times there are neither non-criminal activities nor an awareness space that help explain these offenders' travelling patterns. They commit crimes over large areas, outside their awareness space, but this cannot be reduced to a lack of an anchor point. Even if they travel for non-criminal reasons, one can hardly argue that they know an area well when they have been there only once. For these offenders, awareness space mechanisms seem to function in another way. They have only been in Belgium for a short period, and have not yet developed a full-scale awareness space here. Their movement patterns look like what Morselli and Royer (2008, p. 8) describe as a desperate search: a distant journey that is caused by a lack of resources in an offender's awareness space, thus creating the need to head for unfamiliar areas. However, in our case, this has less to do with an absolute lack of resources, but is more closely related to the fact that their spatial awareness is not yet fully developed. As a result, their awareness space is absent, or at least too small to locate potential targets, forcing them to rely on other characteristics of target areas. These are rather abstract and refer to a general perception of affluence or low risk. Using these general features, they manage to create some sort of mental map. The usage of such a mental map is not new (Nichols, 1980; Rosenbaum &

Lavrakas, 1995). However, in our sample this map seems not to be based on concrete information, but rather general ideas and perceptions.

9.4 Conclusion

Routine activities and awareness space play an important role in criminal behaviour. As awareness space helps shape the criminal range, one might assume that a larger awareness space may result in a larger operation area. Previous research has indeed shown that burglars may become mobile when prompted by an extended awareness space (Polisenska, 2008). Yet, spatial awareness is not static. Bernasco (2010) showed that the location of previous residences may further influence offending patterns for a certain time. As this effect becomes less important over time, it indicates that spatial awareness is dynamic. Our research shows that the lack of a clear awareness space can increase offenders' mobility. As they have no clear knowledge of target suitability, they consider abstract elements. In doing so, it appears the awareness space of these offenders does not provide opportunities – as it has been insufficiently developed – but it also does not limit offenders in their criminal behaviour. Incentives to leave known territory are not limited to criminal opportunities. Because these offenders have no clear awareness of the neighbourhood, they think otherwise and choose to travel far because they expect this behaviour to result in more profits and lower risks.

We claim that awareness space is dynamic and, despite the general perceptions of its proportional link between the size of an offender's operation area and his awareness space, the latter may impose restrictions as well. We have found that offenders without a developed awareness space may operate beyond the borders of what would otherwise be expected. However, a number of weaknesses are evident in our work, providing opportunities for future research.

Our sample consisted of a particular group of offenders whose awareness space in Belgium has been still under development and who were more mobile in their offending patterns. We believe mobile offenders and their awareness spaces are a promising sample for research, as the concept of awareness space for these offenders cannot be reduced to knowledge about their home region. Because of the particularity of our sample, we suggest future work to consider other mobile offenders and their spatial awareness, trying to disentangle awareness space and its influence on mobility from our rather specific sample.

Another future line of research could develop the notion of quantifying awareness space patterns. Our analysis has empirically explored movement of individual offenders, but quantitative research in this domain is limited. However, in today's world it is imperative to corroborate such findings through measurement and quantification. Bernasco (2010) began this through an investigation of residential history and how it helps to shape the operation area. He found that the effect of residential history diminishes over time, which pinpoints another relevant issue. The concept of awareness space has rarely been considered a dynamic concept. Yet, it evolves over time, as people's lives take certain turns. Although this chapter shows that underdevelopment of awareness can lead offenders to offend further away from their homes, awareness development in itself has not been discussed. Given the notable findings in our sample with regards to limited spatial awareness, future work could emphasis how such awareness evolves over time and what that says about offending patterns and their evolution.

Our findings suggest that our understanding of the role of awareness space should be differentiated. We do not question the existence of the concept or its importance. However, we do suggest that spatial awareness does not only provide opportunities for crime, but can actually limit it at times. Offenders who lack a thorough development of such awareness may act according to different principles than those who do not. If spatial awareness of offenders has not reached a certain critical size, it may be that they operate beyond the borders of their (limited) awareness space. Thus, although the size of a criminal's awareness space may provide opportunities for offending, it may also create limitations in the operation area, since people may look only for possible targets within this area. If they lack such awareness, they are not bound by their perceptions of targets and are likely to consider other elements. In other words, they are less bound to what they know and may choose to travel further in their criminal operations. A 'desperate search'? Not really, more a different way of reasoning that is not hampered by a given spatial awareness.

Afterword

The various chapters in this book deal with certain elements which contribute to what is known about offender mobility. Using the case study of so-called 'itinerant crime groups', the scope of the research exceeds the traditionally observed local, urban crime patterns. Although this case study may be of particular interest in Western Europe, certain types of mobile offenders have been observed elsewhere too and some regions even suffer from rather similar crime groups (e.g. Caputo, 2008).

One may criticize the fact that nationality is selected as a study variable. We do realise that nationality itself is not a root cause of mobility, but may refer to other features, such as embedment in a certain region. However, we have observed empirically that from the list of considered variables, nationality makes the largest difference. Therefore, it is a justified choice to work with such a selection. The empirical results of the study have shown us right, as a lot of valuable information was revealed.

Having demonstrated the clear existence of mobile crime patterns, future work could focus on studying mobile offenders in general and revealing their patterns. We believe this work, using a case study, may have opened researchers' perspective on offender mobility. Much important work has been done in the area of urban crime. Furthermore, technological evolutions and computer capacities have given us the possibility to start working with ever smaller geographic units of analysis (Oberwittler & Wikström, 2009). This evolution has demonstrated its value for sure. Yet, similar evolutions also enable us to extend our view, not necessarily by using smaller units of analysis but by grasping larger geographic areas too.

In chapter 8, a chapter in which the focus was not on itinerant crime groups, but on outbound offenders in general, we have demonstrated that nearly half of the crimes are so-called outbound offences. Despite the continuing focus on urban crime and the attraction of cities as criminal opportunity structures (Pyle et al., 1974), such a focus limits a researcher's view to just over one half of the crimes. It shows that the number of potential opportunities alone does insufficiently explain criminal behaviour. Various theoretical considerations deal with offending patterns and offender mobility. Yet, by (nearly) exclusively focusing on those urban patterns, the threat of entering a vicious circle is not unrealistic. The book here has demonstrated that it is worthwhile to take a bit more distance. Not only literally, but also in a way that looking at the bunch of work in the area of geographic criminology brings up some sort of funnel effect. The chapters of this book point out that it is worthwhile to step out of the funnel now and then.

This is not at all to say that the study of urban crime has little value. On the contrary, the study of cities has given criminologists the possibility to explore and understand some important mechanisms in the geography of crime and offending behaviour. However, we are convinced that the results of this study should enable us to take things further. Only by testing theoretical frameworks to the totality of empirical findings in relation to crime patterns can one truly understand the general principles of how crime unfolds. For offender mobility, this not only refers to the target, but also to the anchor point and the path to reach the target. In this way, we hope to have contributed to such a movement that broadens the criminologists view and considers alternative methods, samples and – consequently – findings now and then.

References

Alison, L., Smith, M., & Morgan, K. (2003). Interpreting the accuracy of offender profiles. *Psychology Crime & Law, 9*(2), 185-195.

Andresen, M., & Felson, M. (2010). The impact of co-offending. *British Journal of Criminology, 50*(1), 66-81.

Augustus, L. (2000). De mythe van de bokkerijders. *Maasgouw, 119*(4), 265-274.

Bachman, R., & Schutt, R. (2008). *Fundamentals of research in criminology and criminal justice*. Los Angeles: Sage.

Balthau, M. (2006). Rondtrekkende dadergroepen: naar een geïntegreerde en integrale aanpak. In B. De Ruyver (Ed.), *Rondtrekkende dadergroepen: grensoverschrijdend beleid* (pp. 53-58). Brussel: Politeia.

Barker, M. (2000). The criminal range of small-town burglars. In D. Canter & L. J. Alison (Eds.), *Profiling property crimes* (pp. 57-73). Aldershot: Ashgate.

Beauregard, E., Proulx, J., & Rossmo, K. (2005). Spatial patterns of sex offenders: theoretical, empirical, and practical issues. *Aggression and Violent Behavior, 10*(5), 579-603.

Beavon, D., Brantingham, P., & Brantingham, P. (1994). The influence of street networks on the patterning of property offenses. In R. Clarke (Ed.), *Crime Prevention Studies* (Vol. II, pp. 115-148). Monsey: Criminal Justice Press.

Bennett, T., & Wright, R. (1984). *Burglars on burglary*. Aldershot: Gower.

Bernasco, W. (2004). Een kennismaking met Herman: geografische daderprofilering en ruimtelijke gelegenheidsstructuur. *Tijdschrift voor Criminologie, 46*(1), 2-17.

Bernasco, W. (2006). Co-offending and the choice of target areas in burglary. *Journal of Investigative Psychology and Offender Profiling, 3*(3), 139-155.

Bernasco, W. (2007a). Foerageerstrategieën van Homo Criminalis: Wat kunnen we leren van de gedragsecologie? *Tijdschrift voor Criminologie, 49*(3), 265-276.

Bernasco, W. (2007b). The usefulness of measuring spatial opportunity structures for tracking down offenders: A theoretical analysis of geographic offender profiling using simulation studies. *Psychology Crime & Law, 13*(2), 155-171.

Bernasco, W. (2009). Foraging strategies of homo criminalis: lessons from behavioral ecology. *Crime Patterns and Analysis, 2*(1), 5-16.

Bernasco, W. (2010). A sentimental journey to crime: effects of residential history on crime location choice. *Criminology, 48*(2), 389-417.

Bernasco, W., & Block, R. (2009). Where offenders choose to attack: a discrete choice model of robberies in Chicago. *Criminology, 47*(1), 93-130.

Bernasco, W., & Elffers, H. (2010). Statistical analysis of spatial crime data. In A. Piquero & D. Weisburd (Eds.), *Handbook of quantitative criminology* (pp. 699-724). Dordrecht: Springer.

Bernasco, W., & Luykx, F. (2003). Effects of attractiveness, opportunity and accessibility to burglars on residential burglary rates of urban neighborhoods. *Criminology, 41*(3), 981-1001.

Bernasco, W., & Nieuwbeerta, P. (2005). How do residential burglars select target areas? A new approach to the analysis of criminal location choice. *British Journal of Criminology, 45*(3), 296-315.

Besson, J.-L. (2004). *Les cartes du crime*. Paris: PUF.

Black, C., Vander Beken, T., Frans, B., & Paternotte, M. (2001). *Reporting on organised crime: a shift from description to explanation in the Belgian Annual Report on organised crime*. Antwerpen: Maklu.

Blok, A. (1992). *De bokkerijders: roversbenden en geheime genootschappen in de landen van Overmaas (1730-1774)*. Amsterdam: Prometheus.

Bottoms, A., & Wiles, P. (1992). Explanations of crime and place. In D. Evans, N. Fyfe & D. Herbert (Eds.), *Crime, Policing and Place: Essays in environmental criminology* (pp. 11-35). London: Routledge.

Bottoms, A., & Wiles, P. (2002). Environmental criminology. In M. Maguire, R. Morgan & R. Reiner (Eds.), *The Oxford handbook of criminology* (pp. 620-656). Oxford: Oxford University Press.

Bovenkerk, F. (2001). *Misdaadprofielen*. Amsterdam: Meulenhoff.

Bowers, K., & Johnson, S. (2005). Domestic burglary repeats and space-time clusters. *European Journal of Criminology, 2*(1), 67-92.

Bowling, B., & Foster, J. (2002). Policing and the police. In M. Maguire, R. Morgan & R. Reiner (Eds.), *The Oxford handbook of criminology* (3 ed., pp. 980-1033). Oxford: Oxford University Press.

Brantingham, P., & Brantingham, P. (1981a). Introduction: the dimensions of crime. In P. Brantingham & P. Brantingham (Eds.), *Environmental crime* (pp. 7-26). Beverly Hills: Sage.

Brantingham, P., & Brantingham, P. (1981b). Notes on the geometry of crime. In P. Brantingham & P. Brantingham (Eds.), *Environmental criminology* (pp. 27-54). Beverly Hills: Sage.

Brantingham, P., & Brantingham, P. (1984a). Burglar mobility and crime prevention planning. In R. Clarke & T. Hope (Eds.), *Coping with Burglary* (pp. 77-95). Dordrecht: Kluwer.

Brantingham, P., & Brantingham, P. (1984b). *Patterns in crime*. New York: Macmillan.

Brantingham, P., & Brantingham, P. (1993a). Environment, routine and situation: toward a pattern theory of crime. In R. Clarke & M. Felson (Eds.),

Routine Activity and Rational Choice (pp. 259-294). New Brunswick: Transaction Publishers.

Brantingham, P., & Brantingham, P. (1993b). Nodes, paths and edges: considerations on the complexity of crime and the physical environment. *Journal of Environmental Psychology, 13*(1), 3-28.

Brantingham, P., & Brantingham, P. (1995). Criminality of place: crime generators and crime attractors. *European Journal on Criminal Policy and Research, 3*(3), 5-26.

Brown, B., & Altman, I. (1981). Territoriality and residential crime: a conceptual framework. In P. Brantingham & P. Brantingham (Eds.), *Environmental Criminology* (pp. 55-76). Beverly Hills: Sage.

Brown, M. (1982). Modelling the spatial distribution of suburban crime. *Economic Geography, 58*(3), 247-261.

Bruggeman, W. (2007). Mobiliteit vanuit daderperspectief, benaderd vanuit een criminologisch en politioneel perspectief. In L. Vandenhove (Ed.), *Integrale Veiligheid: mobiliteit* (pp. 163-196). Brussel: Politeia.

Bruggeman, W., De Ruyver, B., & Zanders, P. (1991). *Grensoverschrijdende criminaliteit*. Gent: R.U.Gent - School voor Criminologie.

Bruinsma, G. (2000). *Geografische mobiliteit en misdaad*. Leiden: Universiteit Leiden.

Bruinsma, G. (2004). Misdaaddreigingen uit de nieuwe lidstaten van de EU. *Justitiële Verkenningen, 30*(6), 36-50.

Bruinsma, G. (2007). Urbanization and urban crime: Dutch geographical and environmental research. In M. Tonry (Ed.), *Crime and Justice in the Netherlands* (Vol. 35, pp. 453-502). Chicago: Chicago University Press.

Bruinsma, G., & Bernasco, W. (2004). Criminal groups and transnational markets: a more detailed examination on the basis of social network theory. *Crime Law and Social Change, 41*(1), 79-94.

Buettner, T., & Spengler, H. (2001). Local determinants of crime and criminal mobility: an empirical study using German municipality data. from http://www.uni-magdeburg.de/vfs2002/vfs2001/paper-handling/papers/HannesSpengler.pdf

Canter, D. (2005). Confusing operational predicaments and cognitive explorations: comments on Rossmo and Snook et al. *Applied Cognitive Psychology, 19*(5), 663-668.

Canter, D., & Alison, L. J. (Eds.). (2000a). *Profiling property crimes*. Aldershot: Ashgate.

Canter, D., & Alison, L. J. (Eds.). (2000b). *The social psychology of crime: groups, teams and networks* (Vol. 3). Aldershot: Ashgate.

Canter, D., & Gregory, A. (1994). Identifying the residential location of serial rapists. *Journal of the Forensic Sciency Society, 34*(3), 169-175.

Canter, D., & Hammond, L. (2006). A comparison of the efficacy of different decay functions in geographical profiling for a sample of US serial killers. *Journal of Investigative Psychology and Offender Profiling, 3*(2), 91-103.

Canter, D., & Hammond, L. (2007). Prioritizing burglars: comparing the effectiveness of geographical profiling methods. *Police Practice and Research, 8*(4), 371-384.

Canter, D., & Larkin, P. (1993). The environmental range of serial rapists. *Journal of Environmental Psychology, 13*(1), 63-69.

Canter, D., & Youngs, D. (2008a). Geographical offender profiling: applications and opportunities. In D. Canter & D. Youngs (Eds.), *Applications of geographical offender profiling* (pp. 3-24). Aldershot: Ashgate.

Canter, D., & Youngs, D. (2008b). Geographical offender profiling: origins and principles. In D. Canter & D. Youngs (Eds.), *Principles of geographical offender profiling* (pp. 1-18). Aldershot: Ashgate.

Capone, D., & Nichols, W. (1975). Crime and distance: an analysis of offender behavior in space. *Proceedings of the Association of American Geographers, 7*(1), 45-49.

Capone, D., & Nichols, W. (1976). Urban structure and criminal mobility. *American Behavioral Scientist, 20*(2), 199-213.

Caputo, D. (2008). The South American theft groups: an overview of a transnational criminal network and strategies for field enforcement. *Police Quarterly, 11*(3), 271-288.

Carter, R., & Hill, K. (1980). Area-images and behavior: an alternative perspective for understanding urban crime. In D. Georges-Abeyie & K. Harries (Eds.), *Crime: a spatial perspective* (pp. 193-204). New York: Columbia University Press.

Chainey, S. (2005). Methods and techniques for understanding crime hot spots. In J. Eck, S. Chainey, J. Cameron, M. Leitner & R. Wilson (Eds.), *Mapping crime: understanding hot spots* (pp. 15-21). Washington: National Institute of Justice.

Chainey, S., Tompson, L., & Uhlig, S. (2008). The utility of hotspot mapping for predicting spatial patterns of crime. *Security Journal, 21*(1-2), 4-28.

Clare, J., Fernandez, J., & Morgan, F. (2009). Formal evaluation of the impact of barriers and connectors on residential burglars' macro-level offending location choices. *Australian and New Zealand Journal of Criminology, 42*(2), 132-158.

Clinard, M. (1944). Rural criminal offenders. *The American Journal of Sociology, 50*(1), 38-45.

Cohen, L., & Cantor, D. (1981). Residential Burglary in the United-States - Life-Style and Demographic-Factors Associated with the Probability of Victimization. *Journal of Research in Crime and Delinquency, 18*(1), 113-127.

Cohen, L., & Felson, M. (1979). Social change and crime rate trends: a routine activity approach. *American Sociological Review, 44*(4), 588-608.

Cohen, L., & Felson, M. (1981). Modeling Crime Trends - a Criminal Opportunity Perspective. *Journal of Research in Crime and Delinquency, 18*(1), 138-164.

Cornish, D., & Clarke, R. (1986a). Introduction. In D. Cornish & R. Clarke (Eds.), *The reasoning criminal : rational choice perspectives on offending* (pp. 1-16). New York: Springer.

Cornish, D., & Clarke, R. (Eds.). (1986b). *The reasoning criminal : rational choice perspectives on offending*. New York: Springer.

Costanzo, M., Halperin, W., & Gale, N. (1986). Criminal mobility and the directional component in journeys to crime. In R. Figlio, S. Hakim & G. Rengert (Eds.), *Metropolitan crime patterns* (pp. 73-95). Monsey: Criminal Justice Press.

Cromwell, P., Olson, J., & Avary, D. A. W. (1991). *Breaking and entering: an ethnographic analysis of burglary*. Newbury Park: Sage.

Crott, J. (1990). Bokkerijders in genealogisch perspectief: de vildersfamilie Ponts-Bemelmans uit Hoensbroek. *Maaslandse Sprokkelingen, 12*(1), 1-20.

De Cock, K. (2006a). De rondtrekkende daders aan het woord. In B. De Ruyver (Ed.), *Rondtrekkende daders: grensoverschrijdend beleid* (pp. 45-51). Brussel: Politeia.

De Cock, K. (2006b). Professionele dievenbendes: een terugkerende uitdaging! De veiligheidsketen inzake de aanpak van rondtrekkende daders (Deel 1 - beeldvorming). *Politiejournaal-Politieofficier*(4), 20-24.

De Cock, K. (2007). Rondtrekkende daders: wie zijn ze, wat drijft hen? *Politiejournaal-Politieofficier*(2), 6-9.

De Poot, C., Luykx, F., Elffers, H., & Dudink, C. (2005). Hier wonen en daarplegen? Sociale grenzen en locatiekeuze. *Tijdschrift voor Criminologie, 47*(3), 255-268.

De Raedt, E. (2005). Reizen om te stelen... Logboek van het project rondtrekkende dadergroepen (IV en laatste deel). *Politiejournaal-Politieofficier*(9), 18-22.

De Raedt, E. (2006a). Beeldvorming inzake dievenbendes: let's have insight to see inside. In B. De Ruyver (Ed.), *Rondtrekkende dadergroepen: grensoverschrijdend beleid* (pp. 23-26). Brussel: Politeia.

De Raedt, E. (2006b). Rondtrekkende daders: dynamiek in de criminele markt. In B. De Ruyver (Ed.), *Rondtrekkende dadergroepen: grensoverschrijdend beleid* (pp. 39-44). Brussel: Politeia.

De Raedt, E., Henin, P., Wick, A., Libois, O., & Rokegem, M. (2007). Professionele dievenbendes: een terugkerende uitdaging! De veiligheidsketen inzake de aanpak van rondtrekkende daders (Deel 6: het belang van degelijke gerechtelijk werk). *Politiejournaal-Politieofficier*(3), 12-16.

De Ruyver, B. (2001, 30/07). Law & Order: De bokkenrijders, *De Standaard*.

De Ruyver, B. (2006a). Ten geleide. In B. De Ruyver (Ed.), *Rondtrekkende dadergroepen: Grensoverschrijdend beleid* (pp. 5-8). Brussel: Politeia.

De Ruyver, B. (Ed.). (2006b). *Rondtrekkende dadergroepen: grensoverschrijdend beleid*. Brussel: Politeia.

Deakin, J., Smithson, H., Spencer, J., & Medina-Ariza, J. (2007). Taxing on the streets: understanding the methods and process of street robbery. *Crime Prevention and Community Safety, 9*(1), 52-67.

Denscombe, M. (1998). *The good research guide for small-scale social research projects*. Buckingham: Open University Press.

Dienst voor het Strafrechtelijk Beleid. (2005). *Jaarrapport 2005: georganiseerde criminaliteit in België 2003-2004*. Brussel: Politeia.

Dienst voor het Strafrechtelijk Beleid. (2007). *Jaarrapport 2007: georganiseerde criminaliteit in België 2005-2006*. Brussel: Politeia.

Dortans, H. (2007). *Jahresbericht 2006: Eigentums- und Waffenkriminalität*. Düsseldorf: LKA Nordrhein-Westfalen.

Dupuis, B. (2004). Rondtrekkende dadergroeperingen: de zon komt op in het oosten... *Inforevue*(Juni), 34-37.

Easton, S., & Karaivanov, A. (2009). Understanding optimal criminal networks. *Global Crime, 10*(1-2), 41-65.

Eck, J., & Weisburd, D. (1995). Crime places in crime theory. In J. Eck & D. Weisburd (Eds.), *Crime and place* (pp. 1-33). Monsey: Criminal Justice Press.

Edwards, M., & Grace, R. (2006). Analysing the offence locations and residential base of serial arsonists in New Zealand. *Australian Psychologist, 41*(3), 219-226.

Elffers, H. (2003). Veelplegers of vaakplegers? *Tijdschrift voor Criminologie, 45*(2), 119-126.

Elffers, H. (2004). Decision models underlying the journey to crime. In G. Bruinsma, H. Elffers & J. De Keijser (Eds.), *Punishment, places and perpetrators: developments in criminology and criminal justice research* (pp. 182-195). Cullompton: Willan Publishing.

Elffers, H., Reynald, D., Averdijk, M., Bernasco, W., & Block, R. (2008). Modelling crime flow between neighbourhoods in terms of distance and of intervening opportunities. *Crime Prevention and Community Safety, 10*(2), 85-96.

Felson, M. (2002). *Crime and everyday life* (3 ed.). Thousand Oaks: Sage.

Felson, M. (2003). The process of co-offending. In M. Smith & D. Cornish (Eds.), *Theory for Practice in Situational Crime Prevention* (Vol. 16, pp. 149-167). Monsey: Criminal Justice Press.

Felson, M. (2006a). *Crime and nature*. Thousand Oaks: Sage.

Felson, M. (2006b). *The ecosystem for organized crime*. Helsinki: Heuni.

Felson, M., & Cohen, L. (1980). Human ecology and crime: a routine-activity approach. *Human Ecology, 8*(4), 389-406.

Ferwerda, H., Kleemans, E., Korf, D., & Van der Laan, P. (2003). Veelplegers. *Tijdschrift voor Criminologie, 45*(2), 110-118.

Ferwerda, H., Versteegh, P., & Beke, B. (1995). De harde kern van jeugdige criminelen. *Tijdschrift voor Criminologie, 37*(2), 138-152.

Fijnaut, C. (1998). De mobiliteit van daders en internationale strafrechtelijke samenwerking in de Europese Unie : een schets van het probleem *Liber amicorum Roger Blanpain* (pp. 3-14). Brugge: Die Keure.

Fink, G. (1969). Einsbruchstatorte vornehmlich an einfallstrassen? *Kriminalistik, 23*, 358-360.

FOD Justitie, FOD Kanselarij van de Eerste Minister, & FOD Binnenlandse zaken. (2007). *De aanpak van de rondtrekkende dadergroeperingen: een actualisatie.* Brussel: Federale Politie.

Fritzon, K. (2001). An examination of the relationship between distance travelled and motivational aspects of firesetting behaviour. *Journal of Environmental Psychology, 21*(1), 45-60.

Gabor, T., & Gottheil, E. (1984). Offender Characteristics and Spatial Mobility - an Empirical Study and Some Policy Implications. *Canadian Journal of Criminology, 26*(3), 267-281.

Garland, J., & Chakraborti, N. (2007). 'Protean times'?: Exploring the relationships between policing, community and 'race' in rural England. *Criminology and Criminal Justice, 7*(4), 347-365.

Gerring, J. (2007). *Case study research: principles and practices.* New York: Cambridge University Press.

Goodwill, A., & Alison, L. (2006). The development of a filter model for prioritizing suspects in burglary offences. *Psychology Crime & Law, 12*(4), 395-416.

Groff, E. (2007). Simulation for theory testing and experimentation: An example using routine activity theory and street robbery. *Journal of Quantitative Criminology, 23*(2), 75-103.

Groff, E. (2008). Adding the temporal and spatial aspects of routine activities: a further test of routine activity theory. *Security Journal, 21*(1-2), 95-116.

Groff, E., & McEwen, T. (2006). Visualization of spatial relationships in mobility research: a primer (p. 61). Alexandria: Institute for Law and Justice.

Hakim, S., Rengert, G., & Shachmurove, Y. (2000). Knowing your odds: home burglary and the odds ratio (p. 23): Carress working paper.

Hakim, S., Rengert, G., & Shachmurove, Y. (2001). Target search of burglars: a revised economic model. *Papers in Regional Science, 80*(2), 121-137.

Hardyns, W., & Pauwels, L. (2009). The geography of social cohesion and crime at the municipality level. In M. Cools, S. De Kimpe, B. De Ruyver, M. Easton, L. Pauwels, P. Ponsaers, G. Vande Walle, T. Vander Beken, F. Vander Laenen & G. Vermeulen (Eds.), *Contemporary issues in the empirical study of crime* (pp. 157-178). Antwerp: Maklu.

Harries, K., & LeBeau, J. (2007). Issues in the geographic profiling of crime: review and commentary. *Police Practice and Research, 8*(4), 321-333.

Hesseling, R. (1992a). Dadermobiliteit: een eerste verkenning. *Tijdschrift voor Criminologie, 34*(2), 98-114.

Hesseling, R. (1992b). Using data on offender mobility in ecological research. *Journal of Quantitative Criminology, 8*(1), 95-112.

Hignett, K. (2004). Organised crime in East Central Europe: The Czech Republic, Hungary and Poland. *Global Crime, 6*(1), 70-83.

Hodgson, B., & Costello, A. (2006). The prognostic significance of burglary in company. *European Journal of Criminology, 3*(1), 115-119.

Huisman, S., & Van der Laan, F. (2005). Mobiel banditisme: ongestraft of afgestraft? *Het Tijdschrift voor Politie*(3), 20-24.

J.I.R. (2009, 10/03). Belg pendelt graag naar zijn werk, *De Standaard*.

James, Z. (2007). Policing marginal spaces: controlling gypsies and travellers. *Criminology and Criminal Justice, 7*(4), 367-389.

Johnson, S., & Bowers, K. (2004). The burglary as clue to the future: The beginnings of prospective hot-spotting. *European Journal of Criminology, 1*(2), 237-255.

Johnson, S., Summers, L., & Pease, K. (2009). Offender as forager? a direct test of the boost account of victimization. *Journal of Quantitative Criminology, 25*(2), 181-200.

Kadernota Integrale Veiligheid. (2004). Ministerraad 30-31/03.

Kent, J., Leitner, M., & Curtis, A. (2006). Evaluating the usefulness of functional distance measures when calibrating journey-to-crime distance decay functions. *Computers Environment and Urban Systems, 30*(2), 181-200.

Kleemans, E. (1996). *Strategische misdaadanalyse en stedelijke criminaliteit*. Enschede: Universiteit Twente.

Kleemans, E., Korf, D., & Staring, R. (2008). Mensen van vlees en bloed: kwalitatief onderzoek in de criminologie. *Tijdschrift voor Criminologie, 50*(4), 323-336.

Kocsis, R., Cooksey, R., Irwin, H., & Allen, G. (2002). A further assessment of 'circle theory' for geographic psychological profiling. *Australian and New Zealand Journal of Criminology, 35*(1), 43-62.

Kocsis, R., & Harvey, I. (1997). An analysis of spatial patterns in serial rape, arson, burglary: the utility of the circle theory of environmental range for psychological profiling. *Psychiatry, Psychology and Law, 4*(2), 195-206.

Korps Landelijke Politiediensten. (2008). *Nationaal Dreigingsbeeld 2008: georganiseerde criminaliteit*. Zoetermeer: KLPD.

Kruize, P. (2007). Analyse van geregistreerde helingzaken. In D. Van de Mheen & P. Gruter (Eds.), *Helingpraktijken onder de loep: impressies van helingcircuits in Nederland* (pp. 33-62). Den Haag: Boom Juridische uitgevers.

Laukkanen, M., & Santtila, P. (2006). Predicting the residential location of a serial commercial robber. *Forensic Science International, 157*(1), 71-82.

Laukkanen, M., Santtila, P., Jern, P., & Sandnabba, K. (2008). Predicting offender home location in urban burglary series. *Forensic Science International, 176*(2-3), 224-235.

Legard, R., Keegan, J., & Ward, K. (2003). In-depth interviews. In J. Ritchie & J. Lewis (Eds.), *Qualitative research practice: a guide for social science students and researchers* (pp. 139-169). London: Sage.

Lovegrove, A. (2000). Proportionality, sentencing and the multiple offender. *Punishment and Society, 2*(4), 453-469.

Lu, Y. (2003). Getting away with the stolen vehicle: an investigation of journey-after-crime. *The Professional Geographer, 55*(4), 422-433.

Lundrigan, S., & Canter, D. (2001a). A multivariate analysis of serial murderers' disposal site location choice. *Journal of Environmental Psychology, 21*(4), 423-432.

Lundrigan, S., & Canter, D. (2001b). Spatial patterns of serial murder: an analysis of disposal site location choice. *Behavioral Sciences and the Law, 19*(4), 595-610.

Lyman, M., & Potter, G. (1997). *Organized crime*. Upper Saddle River: Prentice Hall.

Macdonald, R. (1993). Itinerant crime: an intelligent network (p. 95). London: Home office police department.

Maguire, M., & Bennett, T. (1982). *Burglary in a dwelling: the offence, the offender and the victim*. London: Heinemann.

Malczewski, J., & Poetz, A. (2005). Residential burglaries and neighborhood socioeconomic context in London, Ontario: global and local regression analysis. *The Professional Geographer, 57*(4), 516-529.

Marro, P. (2002). *La délinquance itinérante en France en provenance des PECO*. Paper presented at the International colloquium 'la politique et la gestion de flux migratoires dans la perspective de l'élargissement: sécurité nationale et stabilité sociale, Bratislava.

Matsueda, R., Kraeger, D., & Huizinga, D. (2006). Deterring delinquents: a rational choice model of theft and violence. *American Sociological Review, 71*(1), 95-122.

Mawby, R. (1977). Defensible space: a theoretical and empirical appraisal. *Urban Studies, 14*(2), 169-179.

Mawby, R. (2001). *Burglary*. Cullompton: Willan Publishing.

McIllwain, J. (1999). Organized crime: a social network approach. *Crime Law and Social Change, 32*(4), 301-323.

McIver, J. (1981). Criminal mobility: a review of empirical studies. In S. Hakim & G. Rengert (Eds.), *Crime spillover* (pp. 20-47). Beverly Hills: Sage.

McKeown, T. (2004). Case studies and the limits of the quantitative worldview. In H. Brady & D. Collier (Eds.), *Rethinking social inquiry: diverse tools, shared standards* (pp. 139-167). Lanham: Rowman and Littlefield.

Meaney, R. (2004). Commuters and marauders: an examination of the spatial behaviour of serial criminals. *Journal of Investigative Psychology and Offender Profiling, 1*(2), 121-137.

Mizutani, F., & Jewell, P. (1998). Home-range and movements of leopards (Panthera pardus) on a livestock ranch in Kenya. *Journal of Zoology, 244*(2), 269-286.

Morselli, C., & Royer, M.-N. (2008). Criminal mobility and criminal achievement. *Journal of Research in Crime and Delinquency, 45*(1), 4-21.

Morselli, C., & Tremblay, P. (2004). Criminal achievement, offender networks and the benefits of low self-control. *Criminology, 42*(3), 773-804.

Morselli, C., Tremblay, P., & McCarthy, B. (2006). Mentors and criminal achievement. *Criminology, 44*(1), 17-43.

Naus, R. (2008). The 'bokkenrijders': ghost riders in the Limburg sky. Retrieved 03/10, 2009, from http://crossroadsmag.eu/2008/02/the-%E2%80%98bokkenrijders%E2%80%99-ghost-riders-in-the-limburg-sky/

Nee, C., & Meenaghan, A. (2006). Expert decision making in burglars. *British Journal of Criminology, 46*(5), 935-949.

Newburn, T. (2008). *Handbook of policing* (2 ed.). Cullompton: Willan publishing.

Newman, O. (1976). *Defensible space: crime prevention through urban design*. New York: Collier.

Newton, M., & Swoope, E. (1987). *Geoforensic analysis of localized serial murder: the Hillside stranglers located.*

Nichols, W. (1980). Mental maps, social characteristics, and criminal mobility. In D. Georges-Abeyie & K. Harries (Eds.), *Crime: a spatial perspective* (pp. 156-166). New York: Columbia University Press.

Oberwittler, D., & Wikström, P.-O. (2009). Why small is better: advancing the study of the role of behavior contexts in crime statistics. In D. Weisburd, W. Bernasco & G. Bruinsma (Eds.), *Putting crime in its place: units of analysis in geographic criminology* (pp. 35-59). New York: Springer.

Palmer, E., Holmes, A., & Hollin, C. (2002). Investigating burglars' decisions: factors influencing target choice, method of entry, reasons for offending, repeat victimisation of a property and victim awareness. *Security Journal, 15*(1), 7-18.

Park, R., Burgess, E., McKenzie, R., & Wirth, L. (1925). *The city*. Chicago: University of Chicago Press.

Paulsen, D. (2006). Connecting the dots: assessing the accuracy of geographic profiling software. *Policing-an International Journal of Police Strategies & Management, 29*(2), 306-334.

Paulsen, D. (2007). Improving geographic profiling through commuter/marauder prediction. *Police Practice and Research, 8*(4), 347-357.

Pauwels, L. (2002). *De ene buurt is de andere niet, exploratie van mogelijkheden tot contextualisering van geregistreerde criminaliteit op buurtniveau*. Brussels: VUBPress.

Pettiway, L. (1982). Mobility of robbery and burglary offenders: ghetto and nonghetto spaces. *Urban Affairs Quarterly, 18*(2), 255-270.

Phillips, P. (1972). A prologue to the geography of crime. *Proceedings of the Association of American Geographers, 4*, 86-90.

Phillips, P. (1980). Characteristics and typology of the journey to crime. In D. Georges-Abeyie & K. Harries (Eds.), *Crime: a spatial perspective* (pp. 167-180). New York: Columbia University Press.

Piquero, A., & Brame, R. (2008). Assessing the race-crime and ethnicity-crime relationship in a sample of serious adolescent delinquents. *Crime and Delinquency, 54*(3), 390-422.

Polisenska, A. V. (2008). A qualitative approach to the criminal mobility of burglars: questioning the 'near home' hypothesis. *Crime Patterns and Analysis, 1*(1), 47-60.

Ponsaers, P. (2004). Rondtrekkende dadergroepen: rationele Nederlandse criminologen en irrationele criminelen in Vlaanderen. *Tijdschrift voor Criminologie, Jubileumuitgave*, 15-23.

Prime Minister, Minister of Justice, & Minister of Interior. (2010). *Tackling of interant criminal groups: new challenges*. Brussels: Federal Police.

Pyle, G., Hanten, E., Williams, P., Pearson, A., & Doyle, G. (1974). *The spatial dynamics of crime*. Chicago: University of Chicago.

Rand, A. (1986). Mobility triangles. In R. Figlio, S. Hakim & G. Rengert (Eds.), *Metropolitan crime patterns* (pp. 73-95). Monsey: Criminal Justice Press.

Rattner, A., & Portnov, B. (2007). Distance decay function in criminal behavior: a case of Israel. *Annals of Regional Science, 41*(3), 673-688.

Rengert, G. (1992). The journey to crime: Conceptual foundations and policy implications. In D. Evans, N. Fyfe & D. Herbert (Eds.), *Crime, Policing and Place: Essays in environmental criminology* (pp. 109-117). London: Routledge.

Rengert, G. (2004). The journey to crime. In G. Bruinsma, H. Elffers & J. De Keijser (Eds.), *Punishment, Places and Perpetrators: Developments in Criminology and Criminal Justice Research* (pp. 169-181). Cullompton: Willan Publishing.

Rengert, G., & Pelfrey, W. (1998). Cognitive mapping of the city center: Comparative perceptions of dangerous places. In D. Weisburd & T. McEwen (Eds.), *Crime Mapping and Crime Prevention* (Vol. 8, pp. 193-217). Monsey: Criminal Justice Press.

Rengert, G., Piquero, A., & Jones, P. (1999). Distance decay reexamined. *Criminology, 37*(2), 427-446.

Rengert, G., & Wasilchick, J. (1985). *Suburban burglary: a time and a place for everything*. Springfield: Thomas.

Rephann, T. (1999). Links between rural development and crime. *Papers in Regional Science, 78*(4), 365-386.

Reppetto, T. (1974). *Residential crime*. Cambridge: Ballinger.

Reynald, D. (2009). *Guardianship in action: a theoretical and empirical elaboration of the Routine Activity Concept*. Amsterdam: NSCR.

Reynald, D., Averdijk, M., Elffers, H., & Bernasco, W. (2008). Do social barriers affect urban crime trips? The effect of ethnic and economic neighbourhood compositions on the flow of crime in The Hague, The Netherlands. *Built Environment, 34*(1), 21-31.

Reynald, D., & Elffers, H. (2009). The future of Newman's defensible space theory: linking defensible space and the routine activities of space. *European Journal of Criminology, 6*(1), 25-46.

Rhodes, W., & Conly, C. (1981). Crime and mobility: an empirical study. In P. Brantingham & P. Brantingham (Eds.), *Environmental Criminology* (pp. 167-188). Beverly Hills: Sage.

Rosenbaum, D., & Lavrakas, P. (1995). Self-reports about place: the application of survey and interview methods to the study of small areas. In J. Eck & D. Weisburd (Eds.), *Crime and Place* (pp. 285-314). Monsey: Criminal Justice Press.

Rossmo, K. (1995). Place, space and police Investigations: hunting serial violent criminals. In J. Eck & D. Weisburd (Eds.), *Crime and place* (pp. 217-235). Monsey: Criminal Justice Press.

Rossmo, K. (1997). Geographic profiling. In J. Jackson & D. Bekerian (Eds.), *Offender profiling: theory, research and practice* (pp. 159-175). Chichester: Wiley.

Rossmo, K. (2000). *Geographic profiling*. Boca Raton: CRC Press.

Rossmo, K. (2005). Geographic heuristics or shortcuts to failure?: response to Snook et al. *Applied Cognitive Psychology, 19*(5), 651-654.

Rossmo, K., Thurman, Q., Jamieson, J. D., & Egan, K. (2008). Geographic patterns and profiling of illegal crossings of the southern U.S. border. *Security Journal, 21*(1-2), 29-57.

Ruggiero, V. (1996). *Organized and corporate crime in Europe: offers that can't be refused*. Aldershot: Dartmouth.

Santtila, P., Laukkanen, M., Zappala, A., & Bosco, D. (2008). Distance travelled and offence characteristics in homicide, rape, and robbery against business. *Legal and Criminological Psychology, 13*(2), 345-356.

Sarangi, S., & Youngs, D. (2006). Spatial patterns of Indian serial burglars with relevance to geographical profiling. *Journal of Investigative Psychology and Offender Profiling, 3*(2), 105-115.

Segaert, S. (2006). Criminele processen: heling en buit bij Roemeens rondtrekkende dadergroepen en communicatie bij rondtrekkende dadergroepen. In B. De Ruyver (Ed.), *Rondtrekkende dadergroepen: grensoverschrijdend beleid* (pp. 27-38). Brussel: Politeia.

Shelley, L. (1999). Identifying, counting and categorizing transnational criminal organisations. *Transnational Organized Crime, 5*(1), 1-18.

Sherman, L. (1995). Hot spots of crime and criminal careers of places. In J. Eck & D. Weisburd (Eds.), *Crime and Place* (35-52 ed., pp. 35-52). Monsey: Criminal Justice Press.

Sherman, L., Gartin, P., & Buerger, M. (1989). Hot spots of predatory crime: routine activities and the criminology of place. *Criminology, 27*(1), 27-56.

Siegel, D. (2006). *The Criminal Import/Export between East and West Europe.* Paper presented at the CIROC Seminar 20/12, Amsterdam.

Silverman, D. (2001). *Interpreting qualitative data: methods for analysing talk, text and interaction* (2 ed.). London: Sage.

Smith, W., Bond, J., & Townsley, M. (2009). Determining how journeys-to-crime vary: measuring inter- and intra-offender crime trip distributions. In D. Weisburd, W. Bernasco & G. Bruinsma (Eds.), *Putting crime in its place: units of analysis in geographic criminology* (pp. 217-236). New York: Springer.

Snook, B. (2004). Individual differences in distance travelled by serial burglars. *Journal of Investigative Psychology and Offender Profiling, 1*(1), 53-66.

Snook, B., Canter, D., & Bennell, C. (2002). Predicting the home location of serial offenders: a preliminary comparison of the accuracy of human judges with a geographic profiling system. *Behavioral Sciences and the Law, 20*(1-2), 109-118.

Snook, B., Taylor, P., & Bennell, C. (2004). Geographic profiling: the fast, frugal and accurate way. *Applied Cognitive Psychology, 18*(1), 105-121.

Snook, B., Taylor, P., & Bennell, C. (2005). Shortcuts to geographic profiling success: a reply to Rossmo (2005). *Applied Cognitive Psychology, 19*(5), 665-661.

Snook, B., Zito, M., Bennell, C., & Taylor, P. (2005). On the complexity and accuracy of geographic profiling strategies. *Journal of Quantitative Criminology, 21*(1), 1-26.

Snow, J. (2008). Excerpt from: on the mode of communication of cholera (originally from 1855). In D. Canter & D. Youngs (Eds.), *Principles of geographical offender profiling* (pp. 33-39). Aldershot: Ashgate.

Spapens, T., & Fijnaut, C. (2005). *Criminaliteit en rechtshandhaving in de Euregio Maas-Rijn, 1: De problemen van transnationale (georganiseerde) criminaliteit en de grensoverschrijdende politiële, justitiële en bestuurlijke samenwerking.* Antwerpen: Intersentia.

Stepstone Survey. (2009). Imagine that you find the job of your dreams, but far away from home. How long would you travel to your work and back? Retrieved 04/11, 2009, from https://www.stepstone.be/ueberuns/default.cfm?link=traveltime

Steventon, G. (1996). Defensible space: a critical review of the theory and practice of a crime prevention strategy. *Urban Design International, 1*(3), 235-245.

Stouffer, S. (1960). Intervening opportunities and competing migrants. *Journal of Regional Science, 2*(1), 1-26.

Sutton, M. (1998). Handling stolen goods and theft: a market reduction approach (p. 4). London: Home office research and statistics directorate.

Tillyer, M., & Kennedy, D. (2008). Locating focused deterrence approaches within a situational crime prevention framework. *Crime Prevention and Community Safety, 10*(2), 75-84.

Tita, G., & Griffiths, E. (2005). Traveling to violence: the case for a mobility-based spatial typology of homicide. *Journal of Research in Crime and Delinquency, 42*(3), 275-308.

Tittle, C., & Paternoster, R. (1988). Geographic mobility and criminal behavior. *Journal of Research in Crime and Delinquency, 25*(3), 301-343.

Tobler, W. (1970). A computer movie simulating urban growth in the Detroit Region. *Economic Geography, 46*(2), 234-240.

Townsley, M., Homel, R., & Chaseling, J. (2003). Infectious burglaries: a test of the near repeat hypothesis. *British Journal of Criminology, 43*(3), 615-633.

Tremblay, P. (2004). Searching for suitable co-offenders. In R. Clarke & M. Felson (Eds.), *Routine Activity and Rational Choice* (pp. 17-36). New Brunswick: Transaction Publishers.

Turner, S. (1969). Delinquency and distance. In T. Sellin & M. Wolfgang (Eds.), *Delinquency: Selected Studies* (pp. 11-26). New York: Wiley.

Van Calster, P. (2002). Criminele netwerken en het kleine-wereld-effect: de invloed van sociale relaties op organiseren. *Tijdschrift voor Criminologie, 44*(2), 141-149.

Van Daele, S. (2008). Organised property crimes in Belgium: the case of the 'itinerant crime groups'. *Global Crime, 9*(3), 241-247.

Van Daele, S., Vander Beken, T., & De Ruyver, B. (2008). Rondtrekkende dadergroepen: een empirische toets. *Panopticon, 29*(4), 25-39.

Van de Bunt, H., & Kleemans, E. (2007). *Georganiseerde criminaliteit in Nederland: derde rapportage op basis van de Monitor Georganiseerde Criminaliteit.* Den Haag: Boom Juridische Uitgevers.

Van de Velde, M., Pauwels, L., & Hardyns, W. (2009). Lokale verbondenheid en gemeentelijke spreiding van autodiefstal: een empirische toets vanuit een hedendaagse ecologische criminologie. *Panopticon, 30*(5), 19-37.

Van der Kemp, J., & Van Koppen, P. (2007). Finetuning geographical profiling. In R. Kocsis (Ed.), *Criminal profiling: international perspectives in theory, practice, and research* (pp. 347-364). Totowa: Humana.

Van der Laan, F., & Weenink, A. (2005). *Eindrapportage van het project Polaris: Mobiel banditisme uit Polen en Litouwen.* Zwolle: Korps Landelijke Politiediensten.

Van Geffen, R. (2009). *Itinerant groups target stores in European Union: an urgent cross-border problem.* Leidschendam: Detailhandel Nederland.

Van Koppen, P., & De Keijser, J. (1997). Desisting distance decay: On the aggregation of individual crime trips. *Criminology, 35*(3), 505-515.

Van Koppen, P., De Poot, C., & Van Koppen, V. (2000). Cirkels van delicten: over pleegplaatsen van misdrijven en de woonplaats van de daders. *De psycholoog, 35*(10), 435-442.

Van Koppen, P., & Jansen, R. (1998). The road to robbery: travel patterns in commercial robberies. *British Journal of Criminology, 38*(2), 230-246.

Van Koppen, P., Van der Kemp, J., & De Poot, C. (2002). Geografische daderprofilering. In P. Van Koppen, D. Hessing, H. Merckelbach & H. Crombag (Eds.), *Het recht van binnen: psychologie van het recht* (pp. 237-254). Deventer: Kluwer.

Van San, M., Snel, E., & Boers, R. (2002). *Woninginbrekers en zware jongens: daders uit voormalig Joegoslavië in beeld*. Rotterdam: Risbo.

Verfaillie, K., & Vander Beken, T. (2008). Proachtive policing and the assessment of organised crime. *Policing - An International Journal of Police Strategies & Management, 31*(4), 534-552.

Vermeulen, G., De Busser, E., & Cruysberghs, W. (2003). *Criminaliteit in de Frans-Belgische grensregio*. Antwerp: Maklu.

Versteegh, P., Janssen, J., & Bernasco, W. (2003). Beginners, doorstromers en veelplegers: carrièrecriminaliteit in de politieregio Haaglanden. *Tijdschrift voor Criminologie, 45*(2), 127-139.

Vervaet, R., & Willems, A. (2006). Professionele dievenbendes: een terugkerende uitdaging! De veiligheidsketen inzake de aanpak van rondtrekkende daders (Deel 4: ontraden). *Politiejournaal-Politieofficier*(7), 12-15.

Verwee, I., Ponsaers, P., & Enhus, E. (2007). *Inbreken is mijn vak: textuur en praktijk van woninginbraak*. Den Haag: Boom Juridische Uitgevers.

Virta, S. (2002). Local security management: policing through networks. *Policing - An International Journal of Police Strategies & Management, 25*(1), 190-200.

Vogel, G. (1991). Straatroof in Amsterdam: enkele daders aan het woord over risico's, lucrativiteit en prestige. *Justitiële Verkenningen, 17*(9), 58-75.

Von Lampe, K. (2001). Organisierte Kriminalität unter der Lupe: Netzwerke kriminell nutzbarer Kontakte als konzeptueller Zugang zur OK-Problematik. *Kriminalistik, 55*(7), 465-471.

Von Lampe, K. (2004). Making the second step before the first: Assessing organized crime. *Crime Law and Social Change, 42*(4-5), 227-259.

Wartna, B., & Tollenaar, N. (2004). *Bekenden van Justitie: een verkennend onderzoek naar de 'veelplegers' in de populatie van vervolgde daders*. Den Haag: WODC.

Weerman, F. (2001). *Samenplegen: over criminele samenwerkingsverbanden en groepsvorming*. Nijmegen: Ars Aequi Libri.

Weerman, F. (2003). Co-offending as social exchange: explaining characteristics of co-offending. *British Journal of Criminology, 43*(2), 398-416.

Weir-Smith, G. (2004). Crime mobility: spatial modelling of routine activities of arrestees and substance abusers in South Africa. *GeoJournal, 59*(3), 209-215.

Weisburd, D. (2004). The emergence of crime places in crime prevention. In G. Bruinsma, H. Elffers & J. De Keijser (Eds.), *Punishment, Places and Perpetrators:*

Developments in Criminology and Criminal Justice Research (pp. 155-168). Cullompton: Willan Publishing.

Weisburd, D. (2005). Hot spots policing experiments and criminal justice research: lessons from the field. *Annals of the American academy of political and social science, 599*, 220-245.

Weisburd, D., Bruinsma, G., & Bernasco, W. (2009). Units of analysis in geographic criminology: historical development, critical issues, and open questions. In D. Weisburd, W. Bernasco & G. Bruinsma (Eds.), *Putting crime in its place: units of analysis in geographic criminology* (pp. 3-31). New York: Springer.

Weisburd, D., & Eck, J. (2004). What can police do to reduce crime, disorder, and fear? *Annals of the American academy of political and social science, 593*, 42-65.

White, C. (1932). The relations of felonies to environmental factors in Indianapolis. *Social Forces, 10*(4), 498-509.

White, G. (1999). Neighborhood permeability and burglary rates. *Justice Quarterly, 7*(1), 57-67.

Wiles, P., & Costello, A. (2000). *The 'road to nowhere': the evidence for travelling criminals*. London: Home Office.

Wright, R., & Logie, R. (1988). How young house burglars choose targets. *The Howard Journal of Criminal Justice, 27*(2), 92-104.

Yarwood, R. (2007). The geographies of policing. *Progress in human geography, 31*(4), 447-465.

Yow, V. (2005). *Recording oral history: a guide for the humanities and social sciences* (2 ed.). Walnut Creek: AltaMira press.

Zipf, G. (1949). *Human behavior and the principle of least-effort*. New York: Hafner.

Published in the IRCP-series

1. **Trafficking in migrants through Poland**
   N. Siron, P. Van Baeveghem, B. De Ruyver, T. Vander Beken, G. Vermeulen
   ISBN 978-90-6215-655-9 I 1999 I 326 p.
2. **Een geïntegreerd anti-corruptiebeleid voor België**
   T. Vander Beken, T. Carion, B. De Ruyver
   ISBN 978-90-6215-657-3 I 1999 I 144 p.
3. **Anti-corruptiestrategieën**
   B. De Ruyver, F. Bullens, T. Vander Beken, N. Siron
   ISBN 978-90-6215-712-9 I 1999 I 315 p.
4. **Vermiste en seksueel uitgebuite minderjarigen**
   B. De Ruyver, P. Zanders, G. Vermeulen, G. Derre
   ISBN 978-90-6215-717-4 I 2000 I 300 p.
5. **Measuring organised crime in Belgium. A risk-based methodology**
   C. Black, T. Vander Beken, B. De Ruyver
   ISBN 978-90-6215-749-5 I 2000 I 91 p.
6. **Bescherming van en samenwerking met getuigen**
   N. Siron, G. Vermeulen, B. De Ruyver, Ph. Traest, A. Van Cauwenberge
   ISBN 978-90-6215-753-2 I 2000 I 198 p.
7. **The organisation of the fight against corruption in the member states and candidate countries of the EU**
   T. Vander Beken, B. De Ruyver, N. Siron
   ISBN 978-90-6215-772-3 I 2001 I 410 p.
8. **Reporting on organised crime**
   C. Black, T. Vander Beken, B. Frans, M. Paternotte
   ISBN 978-90-6215-775-4 I 2001 I 125 p.
9. **European data collection on sexual offences against minors**
   G.Vermeulen, F. Dhont, A. Dormaels
   ISBN 978-90-6215-786-0 I 2001 I 210 p.
10. **Een nieuwe Belgische wetgeving inzake internationale rechtshulp in strafzaken**
    G. Vermeulen, T. Vander Beken, E. De Busser, C. Van den Wyngaert, G. Stessens, A. Masset, C. Meunier
    ISBN 978-90-6215-798-3 I 2002 I 421 p.
11. **Strategies of the EU and the US in combating transnational organised crime**
    B. De Ruyver, G. Vermeulen, T. Vander Beken (eds.)
    ISBN 978-90-6215-819-5 I 2002 I 466 p.

12. **Finding the best place for prosecution**
T. Vander Beken, G. Vermeulen, S. Steverlynck, S. Thomaes
ISBN 978-90-6215-841-6 | 2002 | 91 p.
13. **Blueprint for an EU criminal records database**
G. Vermeulen, T. Vander Beken, E. De Busser, A. Dormaels
ISBN 978-90-6215-842-3 | 2002 | 91 p.
14. **Multidisciplinary Drug Policies and the UN Drug Treaties**
B. De Ruyver, G. Vermeulen, T. Vander Beken, F. Vander Laenen, K. Geenens
ISBN 978-90-6215-769-3 | 2002 | 156 p.
15. **BUFALAW-2001. The illegal use of growth promoters in Europe**
J. Sabbe, T. Vander Beken (eds.)
ISBN 978-90-6215-803-4 | 2002 | 232 p.
16. **Gewapend bestuursrecht gescreend**
K. Van Heddeghem, T. Vander Beken, G. Vermeulen, B. De Ruyver
ISBN 978-90-6215-822-5 | 2002 | 216 p.
17. **Une nouvelle législation belge d'entreaide judiciaire international en matière pénale**
G. Vermeulen, T. Vander Beken, E. De Busser, C. Van den Wyngaert, G. Stessens, A. Masset, C. Meunier
ISBN 978-90-6215-859-5 | 2003 | 376 p.
18. **Politiecapaciteit in de gerechtelijke zuil. Een methodologische studie**
T. Vander Beken, P. Ponsaers, C. Defever, L. Pauwels
ISBN 978-90-6215-876-8 |2003 | 110 p.
19. **Criminaliteit in de Frans-Belgische grensregio**
G. Vermeulen, E. De Busser, W. Cruysberghs
ISBN 978-90-6215-878-2 | 2003 | 255 p.
20. **Criminalité dans la région frontalière franco-belge**
G. Vermeulen, E. De Busser, W. Cruysberghs
ISBN 987-90-6215-879-2 | 2003 | 251 p.
21. **Internationaal huispersoneel in België – Le personnel domestique international en Belgique**
G. Vermeulen, A. Bucquoye, W. Cruysberghs
ISBN 978-90-6215-885-0 | 2003 | 172 p.
22. **Measuring organised crime in Europe**
T. Vander Beken, E. Savona, L. Korsell, M. Defruytier, A. Di Nicola, A. Heber, A. Bucquoye, A. Dormaels, F. Curtol, S. Fumarulo, S. Gibson, P. Zoffi
ISBN 978-90-6215-939-0 | 2004 (second edition 2006) | 273 p.

23. **Organised crime and vulnerability of economic sectors. The European transport and music sector**
T. Vander Beken (ed.)
ISBN 978-90-6215-820-1 | 2005 | 322 p.

24. **Availability of law enforcement information in the EU. Between mutual recognition and equivalent right of access**
G. Vermeulen, T. Vander Beken, L. Van Puyenbroeck, S. Van Malderen
ISBN 978-90-466-0005-4 | 2005 | 110 p.

25. **EU standards in witness protection and collaboration with justice**
G. Vermeulen (ed.)
ISBN 978-90-466-0006-1 | 2005 | 280 p.

26. **European organised crime scenarios for 2015**
T. Vander Beken (ed.)
ISBN 978-90-466-0027-6 | 2006 | 283 p.

27. **(Strafbare) overlast door jongerengroepen in het kader van openbaar vervoer**
E. De Wree, G. Vermeulen, J. Christiaens
ISBN 978-90-466-0041-2 | 2006 | 348 p.

28. **The SIAMSECT files. Standardised templates and blueprint for EU-wide collection of statistical information and analysis on missing and sexually exploited children and trafficking in human beings**
G. Vermeulen, A. Balcaen, A. Di Nicola, A. Cauduro
ISBN 978-90-466-0072-6 | 2006 | 185 p.

29. **The European waste industry and crime vulnerabilities**
T. Vander Beken (ed.)
ISBN 978-90-466-0105-1 | 2007 | 190 p.

30. **The European pharmaceutical sector and crime vulnerabilities**
T. Vander Beken (ed.)
ISBN 978-90-466-0106-8 | 2007 | 218 p.

31. **Recreatie en (strafbare) overlast**
S. Van Malderen, G. Vermeulen
ISBN 978-90-466-0122-8 | 2007 | 521 p.

32. **Mensenhandel in beeld. Eerste kwantitatieve en kwalitatieve analyse van Belgische slachtofferdata**
G. Vermeulen, E. Van den Herrewegen, L. Van Puyenbroeck
ISBN 978-90-466-0115-0 | 2007 | 487 p.

33. **EU quality standards in support of the fight against trafficking in human beings and sexual exploitation of children**
G. Vermeulen (ed.)
ISBN 978-90-466-0116-7 | 2007 | 444 p.

34. **Developing an EU level offence classification system. EU study to implement the Action Plan to measure crime and criminal justice**
A. Mennens, W. De Wever, A. Dalamanga, A. Kalamara,
G. Kazlauskaitė, G. Vermeulen, W. De Bondt
ISBN 978-90-466-0265-2 I 2009 I 114 p.
35. **EULOCS. The EU level offence classification system: A bench-mark for enhanced internal coherence of the EU's criminal policy**
G. Vermeulen, W. De Bondt
ISBN 978-90-466-0264-5 I 2009 I 112 p.
36. **The MONTRASEC demo. A bench-mark for member state and EU automated data collection and reporting on trafficking in human beings and sexual exploitation of children**
G. Vermeulen, N. Paterson
ISBN 978-90-466-0326-0 I 2010I 156 p.
37. **EU cross-border gathering and use of evidence in criminal matters. Towards mutual recognition of investigative measures and free movement of evidence?**
G. Vermeulen, W. De Bondt and Y. Van Damme
ISBN 978-90-466-0327-0 I 2010I 254 p.
38. **Organised crime involvement in trafficking in persons and smuggling of migrants**
G. Vermeulen, Y. Van Damme and W. De Bondt
ISBN 978-90-466-0344-4I 2010I 112 p.
39. **Nederlandse afhandeling van Belgische rechtshulpverzoeken**
G. Vermeulen and Y. Van Damme
ISBN 978-90-466-0400-7I 2010I 192 p.
40. **Cross-border execution of judgements involving deprivation of liberty in the EU. Overcoming legal and practical problems through flanking measures**
G. Vermeulen, A. van Kalmthout, N. Paterson, M. Knapen, P. Verbeke, and W. De Bondt
ISBN 978-90-466-0455-7 I 2011I 310 p.
41. **Material detention conditions, execution of custodial sentences and prisoner transfer in the EU Member States**
G. Vermeulen, A. van Kalmthout, N. Paterson, M. Knapen, P. Verbeke and W. De Bondt
ISBN 978-90-466-0456-4 I 2011I 1008 p.
42. **Rethinking international cooperation in criminal matters in the EU. Moving beyond actors, bringing logic back, footed in reality.**
G. Vermeulen, W. De Bondt and C. Ryckman
ISBN 978-90-466-0487-8 I 2012

43. **Extending offender mobility. Investigating mobile offenders through the case study of 'itinerant crime groups'.**
S. Van Daele
ISBN 978-90-466-0514-1 | 2012 | 155 p.